Fundraising for Hospitals

Value-Based Healthcare Philanthropy

William J. Mountcastle, MPA

CharityChannel PRESS

Fundraising for Hospitals: Value-Based Healthcare Philosophy

One of the **In the Trenches**™ series

Published by
CharityChannel Press, an imprint of CharityChannel LLC
424 Church Street, Suite 2000
Nashville, TN 37219 USA
charitychannel.com

Copyright © 2017 by CharityChannel Press, an imprint of CharityChannel LLC

All rights reserved. No part of this book shall be reproduced, stored in a retrieval system, or transmitted by any means, electronic, mechanical, photocopying, recording, or otherwise, without written permission from the publisher. No patent liability is assumed with respect to the use of the information contained herein. This publication contains the opinions and ideas of its author. It is intended to provide helpful and informative material on the subject matter covered. It is sold with the understanding that the author and publisher are not engaged in rendering professional services in the book. If the reader requires personal assistance or advice, a competent professional should be consulted. The author and publisher specifically disclaim any responsibility for any liability, loss, or risk, personal or otherwise, that is incurred as a consequence, directly or indirectly, of the use and application of any of the contents of this book. Although every precaution has been taken in the preparation of this book, the publisher and author assume no responsibility for errors or omissions. No liability is assumed for damages resulting from the use of information contained herein.

In the Trenches™, In the Trenches logo, and book design are trademarks of CharityChannel Press, an imprint of CharityChannel LLC, Nashville, Tennessee.

ISBN: 978-1-938077-81-4 hardcover | 978-1-938077-94-4 paperback

Library of Congress Control Number: 2017947005

13 12 11 10 9 8 7 6 5 4 3 2 1

Printed in the United States of America

This and most CharityChannel Press books are available at special quantity discounts for bulk purchases for sales promotions, premiums, fundraising, or educational use. For information, contact CharityChannel Press, 424 Church Street, Suite 2000, Nashville, TN 37219 USA. +1 949-589-5938.

Publisher's Acknowledgments

This book was produced by a team dedicated to excellence; please send your feedback to editors@charitychannel.com.

We first wish to acknowledge the tens of thousands of peers who call *CharityChannel.com* their online professional home. Your enthusiastic support for the **In the Trenches**™ series is the wind in our sails.

Members of the team who produced this book include:

Editors

Acquisitions Editor: Stephen C. Nill

Manuscript Editor: Stephen C. Nill

Production

In the Trenches Series Design: Deborah Perdue

Layout Editor: Jill McLain

Administrative

CharityChannel LLC: Stephen C. Nill, CEO

Marketing and Public Relations: John Millen

About the Author

Bill Mountcastle is the founder and president of Health Giving, a specialized healthcare fundraising consulting firm serving community-based health and healthcare nonprofits. He is a noted expert in healthcare capital campaign planning, collaborative fundraising among major university health science colleges, hospital foundation mergers and strategic restructuring, and grateful patient and physician engagement for fundraising results. He has more than two decades of experience in fundraising, rising to senior leadership positions at leading multispecialty academic medical centers and research universities with sophisticated and successful development programs. He wrote the chapter on healthcare capital campaigns for the 2014 book, *Redefining Healthcare Philanthropy*, from the Association for Healthcare Philanthropy.

Before founding Health Giving, he served as senior associate vice president of development at The Ohio State University. As the chief development officer for the University's Wexner Medical Center and seven health science colleges, he oversaw fundraising activities for all aspects of one of the most comprehensive university health science complexes in the nation. He led efforts to promote interdisciplinary academic, research, and healthcare teams that collaborated closely to optimize philanthropic investments among the seven health science colleges. He helped design and lead quiet phase activities for Ohio State's But For Ohio State capital campaign with a $2.5 billion goal. Prior to joining Ohio State, Mountcastle was vice president of institutional relations and development at University Hospitals Health System in Cleveland, Ohio. In this role, he was also the principal campaign manager for the $1 billion Discover the Difference: The Campaign for University Hospitals, the capital campaign in support of the most comprehensive expansion in the health system's history.

Mountcastle previously had a successful career at The Cleveland Clinic Foundation, rising to senior director of development for the Cleveland

Clinic Heart Center. He helped design and lead the prepublic planning phase of the Clinic's Today's Innovations Tomorrow's Healthcare campaign to raise $1.25 billion, at that time one of the largest campaigns of any not-for-profit academic medical center in the country. He also served as a member of the Clinic's Securing the 21st Century campaign major gift team that successfully raised $256 million, including $148 million in "brick-and-mortar" dollars for a three-building capital campaign, not only exceeding the target but doing so a year ahead of schedule.

A graduate of St. Edward High School, Muskingum College (BA), and Cleveland State University, Levin College of Urban Affairs (MPA), Mountcastle currently serves on the board of the Ohio Association for Healthcare Philanthropy and the development committee for Circle Health Services in Cleveland, Ohio. He has served on the boards of community organizations including the Center for Community Solutions, Down Syndrome Association of Central Ohio, Children's Museum of Cleveland, and Lorain County Habitat for Humanity. *Crain's Cleveland Business* magazine named him to its Forty Under 40 list in November 2007 and *Inside Business* magazine profiled him a One 2 Watch in April 2003.

Dedication

This is for the many philanthropists I have had the pleasure of meeting and working with, who support healthcare organizations with philanthropy so they can provide hope, answers, and, above all, care.

Author's Acknowledgments

First, thanks to my family for having the patience with me for having taken yet another challenge which decreased the amount of time I could spend with them. Most of that work occurred on weekends and other times inconvenient to my family. Especially Jennifer, my wife, who took a big part of that sacrifice, and Clare and Colette, my daughters, who inspire me every day. I hope that when they read this book, they understand why I spent so much time in front of my computer.

Thank you to Connor Hooper for his commitment and collaboration. He played a crucial role. He helped me organize my writing, caught my mistakes, improved my paragraphs and sentences, and suggested ways that bettered my presentation. Thanks, too, to my other Health Giving colleague, Jane Lee, for her helpful brainstorming, skillful proofreading, thoughtful comments, and loyal support.

A general thank you to my many professional mentors, colleagues, coaches, and friends who taught me the ropes of healthcare philanthropy. Their lessons and contributions to my accomplishments are worth mentioning. Although many mentors had enormous influence, one person, in particular, stands out: Sherri Bishop. I worked together with her fundraising for hospitals for ten years, first at the Cleveland Clinic and then at University Hospitals. I am grateful for having had the opportunity to work for and learn from her.

Finally, thanks to Stephen Nill, the publisher at CharityChannel Press, and Jill McLain, the layout editor. Stephen made sure I stayed on the right track. I appreciate his skillful editing and thoughtful guidance. Jill provided important attention to detail to make sure everything looked great. I'm grateful to have worked with both.

Contents

Introduction 1

Chapter One 3
Demonstrating Your Hospital's Value to Clearly Show Impact

Chapter Two 21
Maximizing the Value of Your Hospital's Fundamental Fundraising Programs

Chapter Three 41
Measuring the Value of Your Fundraising to Ensure High Performance and Effectiveness

Chapter Four 53
Investing in Value to Build an Amazing Organization

Chapter Five 71
Sustaining Value to Make a Profound Difference in the Health of Your Community

Chapter Six 85
Concluding Thoughts

Index 91

Summary of Chapters

Chapter One 3
Demonstrating Your Hospital's Value to Clearly Show Impact. The ability to clearly articulate the value of your hospital to the community is vital to attracting and retaining philanthropic investors. In this chapter, I outline how to highlight your hospital's differentiators and utilize multidimensional outreach to demonstrate value to a diverse community of philanthropic investors.

Chapter Two 21
Maximizing the Value of Your Hospital's Fundamental Fundraising Programs. Hospital fundraisers know the fundamentals: prospecting, cultivating, asking, and thanking. And in this chapter, I describe how to significantly enhance a fundraising office through focusing on perfecting just these simple fundamentals.

Chapter Three 41
Measuring the Value of Your Fundraising to Ensure High Performance and Effectiveness. As the old saying goes "if you can't measure it, you can't manage it." Therefore, this chapter will provide specific metrics and methods for strategic planning, assessing performance, and measuring success.

Chapter Four 53
Investing in Value to Build an Amazing Organization. There is value all across your hospital. And too often, value goes unrecognized, uncelebrated, and without investment. This chapter identifies the key value areas within your hospital and fundraising office and explains how to invest in them to build a stronger organization.

Chapter Five 71
Sustaining Value to Make a Profound Difference in the Health of Your Community. This chapter explains the fifth key driver to value-based healthcare philanthropy, sustaining value. Through setting a long-term, future-focused attitude and vision, you can embolden your hospital to overcome obstacles, recognize success, and sustain the support of your community.

Chapter Six 85
Concluding Thoughts. Healthcare is changing faster than ever. And as a hospital fundraiser, you have to be even faster. By focusing on the value-based fundraising outlined in this book, you will position both yourself and your hospital for sustainable success.

Foreword

As a busy philanthropy professional for over thirty years, I am often asked if I have read a certain book on a particular topic. My usual reaction is that those who write many of the books and those with time to read them must not be working on the front lines of philanthropy as I am, or else they wouldn't have the time. For that reason, I am often skeptical of some of the "academic approaches" to this field, which is largely one based not on having advanced degrees in it but on having practical experience and achieving results.

The reader of this book has no such issues to fear when hearing from Bill Mountcastle. I have known Bill for fifteen years and respect him for his capacity to partner with a billionaire on a complex gift to academic medicine as well as work with a rural community hospital foundation on a six-figure gift that is as meaningful to its mission. Bill has a calm, thoughtful, and proven approach to working with those wonderful people in society he describes in this book as "investors" and with the philanthropy professionals, physicians, trustees, and administrators who seek their support. I have seen firsthand how his advice and strategies achieve results.

In this In the Trenches book, you will find the practical tools and inspirational advice to understand the difference between "transactions" and seeking investments from philanthropists by enrolling them in the value-based proposition of your hospital or health system. In today's world of short sound bites and instant gratification from social media postings, Bill reminds us that investors don't want to hear slogans or give to "me too" organizations. They seek to join with hospitals and health systems in changing the world. If your part of the world is an underserved urban center, a complex academic medical center, or a rural hospital where you are the only link to quality healthcare, you will find yourself equipped to dig deep and transform what may have been expressed before as "a good cause" to a vital community asset that is the best investment for a prospective benefactor.

In this concise yet comprehensive work, Bill takes you through an artful balance of depth of purpose and a succinct writing style that covers the waterfront of the most critical aspects of running a healthcare fundraising enterprise. I know this book won't be one of those on your shelf where you never get past the first chapter but one you refer to regularly as you work on the front lines of what I consider a most noble profession: healthcare philanthropy.

John A. Perry, CFRE
Chief Philanthropy Officer
Joslin Diabetes Center
A Harvard Medical School Affiliate

Introduction

At the core of national efforts to improve the quality of healthcare is a shift to value-based care, a drastic transition from the long-standing focus on volume-based healthcare. This market shift toward values-based healthcare, inspired by Harvard economist Michael Porter, is considered revolutionary. The now outdated fee-for-service model had incentives to "do" more. Order more tests. See more patients. Do more procedures. Make more money.

Modern, value-based healthcare is about doing better, not just more. It's about getting good-quality patient outcomes while using fewer healthcare resources; focusing on the continuum of care for patients rather than episodes of care; encompassing qualities of compassion, empathy, and responsiveness to the needs, values, and expressed preferences of the individual patient; employing evidence-based medicine and proven treatments and techniques; viewing the patient as a unique person, rather than focusing strictly on the illness; recognizing that family and friends are essential supports for the patient's healing process; and being transparent, up front, and honest with information so patients can make informed decisions with us.

Healthcare philanthropy is also in a state of transition. Like healthcare professionals, hospital fundraisers are also being asked to challenge assumptions and look for ways to do better instead of just doing more.

And as a healthcare philanthropy professional, I cannot help but draw parallels between the fundamental changes in patient care and in healthcare fundraising. Just like "value-based care" focuses on value, not volume, what I call "value-based healthcare philanthropy" focuses on people, not money.

Working with healthcare systems and hospitals, I see the medical community coming up with strong incentives to encourage doctors to spend more time with their patients, more time educating their patients, and more time listening to their patients and soliciting input when considering various testing and treatment options. Likewise, hospital fundraising teams need to come up with strong incentives to spend more time listening and building relationships with philanthropic investors, learning about philanthropic investor needs and preferences, and building strong personal connections based on trust, responsiveness, and mutual benefit.

I developed a methodology to help hospital fundraising teams succeed with value-based healthcare philanthropy. I strongly believe effective hospital fundraising offices should embrace these five key drivers of value-based philanthropy. They are:

1. Demonstrating your value to clearly show impact

2. Maximizing the value of your core programs

3. Measuring your value to ensure high performance and effectiveness

4. Investing in value to build an amazing organization

5. Sustaining value to make a profound difference in the health of your community

Chapter One

Demonstrating Your Hospital's Value to Clearly Show Impact

IN THIS CHAPTER

- Highlight your hospital's differentiators
- Confirm the tangible difference your hospital makes
- Become indispensable to the community
- Acknowledge perception of value varies

Today, it is critically important to demonstrate value to secure philanthropic investment. So, how do you demonstrate that your hospital's value extends far beyond its building and beds? How do you demonstrate your hospital's value to clearly show impact? You do it by highlighting your hospital's differentiators, confirming the tangible difference your hospital is making to save and improve lives, becoming indispensable to your community, and acknowledging that perception of value varies between different philanthropic investors.

Just declaring your hospital is valuable is not a substitute for actually demonstrating value on a consistent basis. As they say, "actions speak louder than words." Yes, actions are important because demonstrating value is not simply a communications exercise. Your hospital needs to both act and communicate what you are doing. It needs to express what meaningful results you have achieved. It needs to show how investment resulted in community benefit (wellness programs, health programs, research, education, and community health, etc.). It needs to know that your community and your philanthropic investors want to know the motivation behind why, and the details of how, your hospital made a difference. It needs to talk about the things your hospital does that your community and philanthropic investors would say are valuable. It needs to be perceived as making a positive contribution to your community. Your hospital's value is recognized for its importance by the people in the communities through their decision to turn to you for care and for their generous philanthropic investment.

The results of demonstrating value can be financially rewarding and more. Hospitals that demonstrate their value build a positive reputation, attract more patients, secure a viable advantage, engage more and better philanthropic investors, and accrue many other benefits that contribute to greater philanthropic investments.

When your hospital's fundraisers discuss how to demonstrate your hospital's value, their primary focus should be on philanthropic investors. However, the opinions of all community stakeholders matter, from the politicians, referring physicians, payers, activists, news reporters, online reviewers, and others. If your hospital's value is well-regarded by your community and philanthropic investors, they will be more inclined to assist and support you rather than the other organizations vying for their backing. And in turn, they will influence others in the community by word of mouth. And when you effectively demonstrate your value, philanthropic investors, and community stakeholders will be more firm in their support during times of both struggle and success.

This chapter will provide practical and actionable steps for demonstrating your hospital's value to its community. These steps include

- highlighting your hospital's differentiators;
- confirming the tangible difference your hospital is making to save and improve lives;
- becoming indispensable to the community; and
- Acknowledging the perception of value varies between philanthropic investors.

With so many clinicians, service offerings, and care settings, effectively demonstrating value can be overwhelming and cumbersome. To that end, this chapter will also spotlight a few best-practice examples from industry

Philanthropic Investors vs. Charitable Donors

It is more than just semantics. In this book, I refer to *philanthropic investors* and not charitable donors, givers, contributors, patrons, supporters, or benefactors. I do this because I personally believe there is a distinct difference between investing in a hospital and making a gift, offering support, or presenting a contribution. I believe the hospital fundraising process is about getting people to connect to the mission of your hospital, to understand your hospital's success and opportunities, and to get them to commit their dollars by investing in your hospital. These people are not giving or donating, rather they are looking for a return on their investment.

There are a great number of parallel characteristics shared by successful business investors and successful philanthropic investors. They are patient. They are focused and disciplined. They know how to use leverage to their advantage, and, they have a network of friends that share ideas and brainstorm on investment challenges and opportunities. And finally, they are passionate. These characteristics are important to recognize and appreciate, and I strongly believe that a key part of hospital fundraising is learning who your investors are, what they value, and what return on investment they expect to see from your hospital.

A hospital philanthropic investor once said to me, "Today, I am making an investment, not a gift. When we attend your annual holiday ball and auction, we might bid $150 on some artwork or baskets—that's giving. But when we make a financial contribution to this hospital, we are investing in something we truly believe in."

Today's philanthropic investors are not giving because of an immediate emotional response to a need, but rather they are seeking out root causes of issues and endeavors to find a solution. They are problem-solving. They have an expectation of a return. They are not just helping to achieve something or giving to a fund or project to meet a campaign goal. They are investing in your hospital's mission, your people, and your value. And investment-minded people keep track of their investments and want to see them grow and thrive. Investors communicate with and motivate their peers. Investors seek connections that will boost their investment's value. And investors are allies in demonstrating your hospital's value.

principle

leaders that can be adapted and utilized at your hospital. These steps and models will help form a focused and strategic guide for your hospital to demonstrate its value.

Highlight Your Hospital's Differentiators

There is always something that differentiates your hospital from all the others in the crowded healthcare landscape. And ensuring that your differentiators are well-defined is an integral part of demonstrating your hospital's value to your community.

Ask yourself: why is your hospital more valuable to your community and to your philanthropic investors than other organizations and causes in the community? Is it because your hospital specializes in clinical innovations and provides the best treatments available? Is it because your hospital is groundbreaking or experimental and may be providing care or research not available elsewhere? Is it because you deliver consistent results or provide the highest standard of care?

Whatever your differentiators are, talk about them often so you stand out among the crowd. And know that your differentiators do not have to be absolutely unique to your hospital. They just need to be unlike most hospitals. Remember, highlight not just who your hospital is but why your hospital is different. Setting your hospital apart from your competitors is critical to demonstrating value to your community and to philanthropic investors. Distinguish your hospital from the others and make sure your differentiators are true, provable, and relevant.

Highlighting your differentiators helps make your hospital's brand and reputation stand out to philanthropic investors. One example might be that because your hospital is comprised of care facilities spread across all parts of the community, you are uniquely able to provide service to patients close to home. Another differentiator may be that your hospital especially high-quality cancer services, with the latest technology and resources to support patient comfort and positive outcomes. Other hospitals do similar work, but if most hospitals or healthcare organizations in your community do not, this is a differentiator.

As healthcare continues to evolve toward a more value-based, patient-centric delivery model, we will see countless examples of hospitals highlighting how their differentiators enhance the patient experience. Many will emphasize offering patients heightened privacy and amenities, many will focus on comfort and satisfaction, including highly personalized services and holistic care offerings. We will also see hospitals highlighting their reputation as being a value maximizer, meaning they provide the best outcomes for their patients' money and seek to reduce unnecessary procedures and costs. More and more, hospitals will emphasize that their differentiator is offering affordable, high-quality care and experience without waste or complexity.

Concentrate on the following three strategic, targeted actions to highlight your differentiators:

1. Showing that you exercise sound business practices
2. Aligning your fundraising and marketing communications
3. Increasing your presence in the community

Show That You Exercise Sound Business Practices

This means operating ethically, with clear principles, and includes having a clear purpose and mission. With philanthropic investors, your hospital needs to be clear about why, how, and what it does, and in a manner meaningful to your community. Purpose guides your hospital. Purpose is the why your hospital does what it does, why your hospital exists, and why it serves its community. Mission drives your hospital. Your hospital's mission is what it does to accomplish its purpose, what difference it makes, and what change it will create. Your hospital's mission is what drives your hospital every day to fulfill its purpose.

But *sound business practice* means more. Beyond mission and purpose, your hospital needs to show it has a strategic plan that is outward, and responsive to the community's healthcare needs and other external factors. Your hospital must substantiate its planning efforts, take into consideration community needs and market research, acknowledge competing healthcare organizations, and utilize other sources of information to ensure that it is not too siloed in its planning efforts.

Exercising sound business practices also means your hospital has an active and informed governance structure, solid fiscal management process in place, and strong leadership running the organization. Many philanthropic investors have high expectations of those working to fulfill your hospital's mission, including talented board members, executive administrators, physicians, staff, and volunteers.

Sound business practice also signifies that your hospital has an active process in place to properly handle governance issues, board nominations, and board term limits. It means having an active strategic plan that is reviewed and adjusted regularly if necessary.

Many believe that sound business practice also means being transparent and undergoing regular and ongoing evaluations of your hospital's programs, welcoming regular community input, and utilizing it to guide continual organizational improvement.

Align Your Hospital Fundraising and Hospital Marketing Communications

The silo mentality may be great for farms, but it is woefully inadequate for demonstrating the value of your hospital to philanthropic investors and your community. It is a mind-set where departments within the same business do not share information.

Hospital branding is vital to communicating value and impact to the community. Your hospital's brand reflects its identity. It brings your hospital's mission statement to life. And when hospitals are separated into marketing and fundraising silos, their brands, identities, and missions are weakened.

Best-practice hospitals have a strong brand identity, speak with a single voice, deliver clear messages that resonate, and do not separate marketing and fundraising into silos. Rather, marketing and fundraising arms work together to create compelling, relevant content to reach and inspire every audience of your hospital, especially philanthropic investors. They collaborate to enhance fundraising while simultaneously and consistently branding their hospital. They sync marketing communications and fundraising. They work together to make people value their hospital's brand and its promise. And most importantly, they create and maintain a branding message that is meaningful to the community they serve.

Hospital fundraising and marketing communications must avoid a lack of communication and encourage cross-departmental support and collaboration. At best-practice hospitals, the two departments work together to demonstrate value and to promote good news as soon as it happens. Whether it's stories about philanthropic investors or exciting new medical advances taking place at your hospital, together, fundraising and marketing teams must keep all audiences informed and enthusiastic about your hospital.

Effective fundraising and marketing departments collaborate on budgets and financial resources to focus on high-priority hospital service lines. They stay united on internal communications, engaging opinion-leading doctors and hospital executives in their processes and informing them of the results. They are always externally focused and working together to create memorable advertising on radio, television, online, direct mail, and community events. They tell fantastic grateful patient and prominent philanthropic investor stories brilliantly. They take advantage of public relations opportunities. And they never forget they are communicating with humans.

Increase Your Presence in the Community

Your hospital's profile in the community is an important factor for philanthropic investors looking to determine your value. Increasing your hospital's presence means making your hospital more visible in your area and more meaningful and valuable to your community. Best-practice hospitals demonstrate their value in publicly noticeable ways. They increase their hospital's presence in their community through a focus on reputation and relationships and proactively search for opportunities to become involved in community groups.

Increasing your hospital's presence has many advantages if done well. But it must be done systematically and strategically to get the best results. From the strategies below, your hospital can develop specialized approaches for increasing its profile in your community.

Best-Practice Approaches

Best-practice approaches to increasing your hospital's presence include the following:

- ◆ Hosting community health fairs or gatherings on health and wellness. These types of events reflect your hospital's commitment to promoting health and wellness. They often include health screenings, blood glucose testing, blood pressure checks, free flu shots as well as preventative education on strokes, injuries, senior safety, nutrition, and cancer. Preventative care and wellness education are key ingredients to the early detection and intervention of potentially life-threatening conditions. To maximize exposure, host these events in the most visible places in your community: the local grocery store, the recreation center, or at a popular park.

- Implementing a weight management program that includes meal replacement program and nutrition coaching. This may include holding monthly cooking classes focused on better nutrition choices with take-home recipes.

- Promoting your hospital's expertise and healthcare experts. This can be done by writing opinion pieces, positioning your hospital's experts as health industry commentators in the media, making your leaders and physicians accessible to journalists, and keeping a hospital spokesperson readily available to give an interesting and different health or medical point of view.

- Striking the right partnerships to raise the hospital's profile. This is done by partnering with those who stand for the same things as your hospital stands for, aligning with the large employers or universities in the community, and/or having hospital leadership seek out and join business networking groups, like the local chamber of commerce, or leadership groups that work to improve the economic vitality of your community.

- Giving the news media information about what your hospital is doing. Press is critical to building up your hospital's profile. This can be done by meeting with the relevant journalists within local media, befriending the right writers, and advertising hospital programs to draw attention to your hospital and get noticed by your community.

- Nominating your hospital leaders for business awards. Many organizations and publications give out annual awards to the prominent leaders of a particular industry. Winning an award can earn your hospital or its leadership coverage in the press, the respect of the community and philanthropic investors.

- Arranging for hospital employees to give back to the community by volunteering for a day of caring or working with community-based organizations. Showing that you are investing in the community is so important and reinforces to your own employees that your hospital is focused on generating positive community impact.

- Being philanthropic or helping another community-based nonprofit to raise philanthropic investment such as a United Way community campaign. Having a hospital leader be one of the driving forces behind a community campaign can be beneficial. It also puts your hospital leader in touch with potential high-profile partners and could open the door to new philanthropic investors in the future.

- ◆ Sponsoring a local sports team or backing a 5K, 10K, marathon, or walking event. Aligning with professional sports teams and other types of health events promotes your hospital's expertise and support other health and wellness initiatives. Sports marketing is a distinctive way to activate your hospital's message, connect with a large audience, and elevate your hospital's profile in the community.

Confirm the Tangible Difference Your Hospital Makes

Brag about generating a return for your philanthropic investors. An old saying goes: "Don't hide your light under a bushel." Drawing attention and sharing the difference your hospital is making is essential to demonstrating value to philanthropic investors. Show achievements and impact in a way that provides insight into performance, such as improvement trends, in relation to your goals, or in relation to a hospital industry or healthcare benchmark. The key is discussing your hospital's achievements in a community-centered way. Remaining community-centered and sharing credit for your hospital's accomplishments is the most effective way to express your value.

The truth is, the hospitals that make their achievements well known are often seen as more competent and making the biggest difference. I am sure your hospital is making real, tangible differences in healing or saving lives, and you need to express that. Make a detailed list of your accomplishments, how your hospital achieved them, and why your hospital is proud. Share the tangible differences your hospital is making by demonstrating how your hospital assists the poor, sick, elderly, and inform in your community. Share how you continue to benefit patients with free care.

As a healthcare philanthropy consultant who has been in hundreds of hospitals around the United States, I have been fortunate to witness a broad array of organizational cultures and learn a great deal from the great people I have met along the way. This broad exposure has also allowed me to observe the good, the bad, and the downright ugly. I have seen firsthand and time again that best-practice hospitals continue to assure their community that they still offer financial assistance to fill gaps in Medicaid underpayments, charge no fees or discounted fees to underinsured, low-income, or medically indigent patients for needed healthcare services, and provide unprofitable healthcare services such as trauma care, burn care, and outreach primary care and preventative services. Do not struggle with the idea of shouting your hospital's difference-making and community benefit achievements from the rooftops.

Always tie your hospital's success back to what it means to your community. For example, talk about how your hospital's support for community-wide health planning efforts, medical education or research, community health education programs, or increasing jobs sends a positive return on investment back to the community and its people. And whenever possible, monetize and express the value of your hospital's activities as a dollar figure for community leaders and philanthropic investors who focus on the financial bottom line. Putting dollar figures on community value is complicated, but best-practice hospitals often develop an estimate of the economic benefits of their hospital's activities through the creation of an economic impact report.

In today's environment, hospitals are expected to make a tangible difference, deliver excellent care, engage with their communities, and demonstrate value to patients, payers, public policymakers, and philanthropic investors.

To confirm the tangible difference your hospital makes,

- tell your hospital's grateful patient stories;
- create a sense of urgency for your hospital's needs;
- show the priority your hospital puts on improving the health of the community; and
- develop a strong "case for philanthropic investment" for your hospital.

Tell Your Hospital's Grateful Patient Stories

The best way to brag about yourself is not to brag at all. The best way is to let others do the bragging for you. Possibly the most persuasive content that a philanthropic investor will utilize to assess the value of your hospital is not the marketing and communications pieces about new facilities, programs, or equipment, it will likely be your grateful patient stories. These stories of struggle, strength, and hope from grateful patients provide a powerful and emotional experience for philanthropic investors as they consider investing in your hospital.

Encourage your hospital's clinicians and fundraising team to be engaged in identifying and sharing grateful patient stories. Everyone at your hospital should proactively collect inspiring stories of gratitude that affirm your hospital's value and your fundraising office should create accessible systems for storing and sharing these stories for future use. Look for inspiring story opportunities within your patient database, including family, friends, and visitors. And be sure to use a mixture of stories that touch upon different parts of your hospital, especially those areas identified as philanthropic priorities.

Why are these grateful patient stories so precious? Because they are honest and genuine reflections of your hospital's impact on actual people. They inspire empathy. They are not promotions. They are not fluffed up with marketing lingo. They are relatable and relevant. They show philanthropic investors why they should care. They convey authenticity. Telling grateful patient stories demonstrates your value and strengthens your hospital's reputation as a caregiver by expressing the very personal trust that individuals in your community have in your hospital.

Make grateful patient storytellers feel welcomed, loved, appreciated, and important. Be transparent about using their story to show impact or to fundraise and always ask and obtain written permission from patients before publishing their stories. Never use a grateful patient's name without their permission and be sure to work with them to find creative ways to shield personal details if they wish to remain unidentified.

You may need to coach a grateful patient a bit to get a good story. But always stay genuine in your storytelling. False claims will simply undermine your hospital. The community and top philanthropic investors will be able to sniff out phony stories. Appreciate that grateful patient stories are one of the best ways to demonstrate value and take the time to identify, record, and utilize your compelling stories to attract philanthropic investors.

> **observation**
>
> If you are interested in finding more guidance on the importance of storytelling, I recommend you read Julia Campbell's book, *Storytelling in the Digital Age: A Guide for Nonprofits.*

Create a Sense of Urgency for Your Hospital's Needs

Often, to demonstrate value, philanthropic investors need some motivation. Creating a sense of urgency is absolutely one way to motivate. Creating urgency is about helping people to see the need for immediate change, and instant investment. Your hospital needs to express that while its challenges are immense, philanthropic support will embolden it to excel past them.

Your community and your philanthropic investors cannot fully respect your hospital's value without acknowledging that they truly need the hospital, so get them to see the big picture. Give your community and your philanthropic investors a push by creating earnestness around the health issues that are impacting the health of your community and your operations, issues such as patient noncompliance, substance abuse, underfunded behavioral health programs, and the impact of chronic disease on hospitalizations and readmissions.

Communicate about healthcare economics, finances, and what is behind bad debt. And although your hospital is making great advances, these considerable financial and health challenges exist in your community. When your hospital helps the community and your philanthropic investors recognize the community's needs, you will create urgency and increase the awareness of value and the likelihood that they will take action immediately to support the community and your hospital. Your hospital will spark motivation and demonstrate value by developing a sense of urgency around your hospital's needs.

Show the Priority Your Hospital Puts on Improving the Health of the Community

To effectively show the priority your hospital puts on improving the health of a community, it is important to understand the needs of the community. This understanding can be achieved through a community needs assessment. And as it happens, the Patient Protection and Affordable Care Act (ACA), amid changing the hospital marketplace by reducing the number of Americans who lack health insurance and expanding health insurance coverage while placing greater emphasis on community health improvement, also requires hospitals that want to qualify for tax exemption conduct a community health needs assessment (CHNA) once every three years. The purpose of the CHNA requirement was not only to identify health problems in the community served by your hospital but also to develop and implement evidence-based plans to address these health problems.

It is well known from these CHNA that many factors influence the health and wellness of a community, and many entities and individuals in the community, not just the hospital, have a role in responding to these community health needs.

However, your hospital best shows the priority it is putting on improving the health of your community by taking a leading role in guiding a comprehensive, community-wide approach to improving health by developing and implementing a strategy for action. Be the problem-solver and philanthropic investors will reward you for it.

Develop a Strong "Case for Philanthropic Investment" for Your Hospital

Your hospital's case for philanthropic investment, sometimes called your "case statement," is one of the most important documents for demonstrating your hospital's value to philanthropic investors. It sets the foundation for all your philanthropic conversations, and is a valuable resource to everyone soliciting investments in your hospital.

Your case for philanthropic investment must clearly illustrate your hospital's mission and, vision for the future. It ought to tell philanthropic investors why your hospital needs funding, what outcomes your hospital is seeking from their investment and offer strong rationale for why prospective philanthropic investors should invest in your hospital. It is important your case share the reasons for "why" your hospital is important and valuable to your community. It is a powerful tool to be used to build deeper relationships with your philanthropic investors.

Strong case statements include a mix of

- your hospital's most emotionally compelling patient care stories;
- captivating descriptions of your hospital's great work; and
- clear facts affirming your reputation as a positive difference maker.

Great hospital case statements help philanthropic investors connect the dots between the act of making a philanthropic investment and the ultimate impact achieved. Use your case statement to build community connections between hospital leaders, physicians, nurses, therapists, philanthropic investors, and patients. And know that the statistics in your case statement are important, but they are meaningless without a connection to the individuals and families your hospital impacts. Provide detailed information on your hospital's programs at a local level and weave your grateful patient stories and vivid graphics into your statistics and figures to add weight to your message.

> **Building a Strong Case**
>
> Here I have just covered some of the basics for developing a strong case for philanthropic investment for your hospital. For additional guidance in developing a strong case, I highly recommend CharityChannel's *Quick Guide to Developing Your Case for Support* by Margaret Guellich and Linda Lysakowski.
>
> 👍 practical tip

Create a robust experience that empowers philanthropic investors to become informed evangelists and builds the sense that each is crucial to the success of your hospital's mission. And each time your hospital produces newsletters, direct mail, digital content, signage, event speeches, videos, or any other media to carry its message, your communications team should constantly be referring to your case statement to ensure alignment with the logic and language used with philanthropic investors and the community.

Become Indispensable to the Community

If your hospital can become indispensable to your community, you are truly demonstrating value. Being indispensable means being reliable, providing innovative ideas, and delivering solutions for your community's health problems. It means not always talking about your hospital's needs or your hospital's budget. Instead, being indispensable means your hospital focuses its attention on making decisions that are in the best interest of your community.

Being indispensable means your hospital acknowledges and leverages the expertise and strengths of all individuals, resources, and programs. It means being especially appreciative of the philanthropic investors whose generosity and support have helped your hospital to build buildings, acquire equipment, develop new patient care programs and train new caregivers.

Being indispensable also means harmonizing, coordinating, and joining forces with many community partners and expanding the possibilities for participation in your success at every level. Finally, it means being the connection between all who contribute to the goal of excellent healthcare and an excellent community. The following action steps will guide your hospital to becoming a truly indispensable community asset.

To become indispensable to your community,

- create opportunities for personal interaction with your hospital;
- be open to feedback; and
- advance new, innovative community health improvement activities.

Create Opportunities for Personal Interaction with Your Hospital

Technology allows us to interact across so many platforms today. Email, texting, instant messaging, and video conferencing are all common tools we use each day. But regardless of what technology we use, all our interactions still rely on a basic element: each other.

No matter how many new and shiny tools we have, we cannot effectively demonstrate our value without engaging individuals in the community face-to-face. Best-practice hospital fundraisers meet community leaders and philanthropic investors in person and spark meaningful dialogues with them. They invite community leaders into their hospitals to meet their clinical leadership teams and see their work firsthand. They take them to the front lines of their hospital programs so they can see the impact.

One best-practice hospital, with the help of two physician leaders, created Immersion Day, a day where community leaders gathered with physician leaders, met patients, observed surgeries, and sat in on post-op family briefings. The physicians reported about this Immersion Day's effectiveness in *The New England Journal of Medicine* in March 2016.

Be Open to Feedback

The key to a successful conversation is simply lending an ear. To become indispensable to your community, listen and pay attention to feedback. By looking to the community and philanthropic investors to identify what is and is not working, and making appropriate adjustments, your hospital can greatly add to its value for the community.

Gather community members' views and opinions through meetings, focus groups, and one-on-one conversations to identify ways to improve healthcare programs and expose service gaps. Gathering this feedback helps avoid the habit of doing only those things that your hospital leaders may like but have little-perceived value by philanthropic investors or the community. And acting on this feedback will build a powerful perception in the mind of your community and philanthropic investors that they matter to your hospital and are a true and meaningful driver of your mission.

Advance New, Innovative Community Health Improvement Activities

To demonstrate value, best-practice hospitals address the top health needs of their community. Best-practice hospitals are demonstrating value by advancing new, innovative community health activities. Examples include

- partnering with city planners to develop safe places for residents to get daily exercise;
- helping support the development of grocery stores or farmer's markets in neighborhoods that lack access to fresh, healthy foods;
- providing asthma patients with special vacuum cleaners and other tools that can help eliminate harmful triggers;
- partnering with senior centers to offer dinner and dance classes to encourage wellness;
- partnering with the Legal Aid Society to help tenants ensure their landlords make repairs to remediate unhealthy or hazardous conditions;
- using geocoding technology to identify the areas of greatest need by mapping resident clusters that are associated with hospital admissions;
- partnering with existing health delivery ventures such as federally qualified health centers (FQHCs) in underserved areas; and
- expanding health insurance coverage into neighborhoods where the conditions make it harder to engage in healthy, disease-preventing behaviors.

Many best-practice hospitals also seek to improve the healthcare workforce to advance community health. Examples of their initiatives include

- supporting high school internship programs to provide exposure to healthcare settings;
- collaborating with schools to offer health fitness education and exercise equipment;
- partnering with high schools to provide training for allied health professions;
- assisting with first responder and EMS training; and
- funding a health career scholarship program.

Not all the activities listed above will apply or be practical for all communities; rather, these ideas should be modified or tailored to fit your community's unique needs or serve as a springboard for new ideas to advance community health. Be entrepreneurial in how you are addressing community health and wellness programs.

Acknowledge the Perception of Value Varies Between Philanthropic Investors

"No Two Alike" was a marketing campaign for an academic health system in Florida. The campaign focused on the personal and intimate stories of individuals who received care at their hospital. The ads ran throughout Florida in print, radio, and on billboards. The gist was that no two patients are alike and that the hospital's physicians develop unique, specialized treatment programs for each patient.

The same approach must be exercised as you approach philanthropic investors—no two are alike. Their opinions of value will vary, and they will evaluate your hospital differently. To be effective, your hospital should separate philanthropic investors to make sure that you are spending your time as wisely as possible. Segment them. Then devise an appropriate engagement plan, creating the basic framework and layering on more personal outreach for philanthropic investors who have invested higher amounts or have the capacity and inclination to invest greater.

Appreciate that philanthropic investors may use emotional, societal, financial, logical, or other criteria to determine value. Philanthropic investors must believe that the exchange of "good feeling" or "social equity" provided through your hospital's mission outcomes is greater than their contribution to your organization. And because no two philanthropic investors are alike, your hospital must segment potential philanthropic investors and create specialized appeals, messages, and recognition for their unique values.

To Recap

◆ Highlight your hospital's differentiators.

◆ Confirm the tangible difference your hospital makes.

◆ Become indispensable to the community.

◆ Acknowledge perception of value varies.

Chapter Two

Maximizing the Value of Your Hospital's Fundamental Fundraising Programs

IN THIS CHAPTER

- ➔ Thank philanthropic investors extraordinarily
- ➔ Ask philanthropic investors effectively
- ➔ Prospect for new philanthropic investors thoroughly
- ➔ Establish beneficial community partnerships

Hall of Fame basketball coach John Wooden made sports history in 1973 by becoming the first coach in any major sport to win seven consecutive national championships. Over the course of his career, Wooden won a total of ten championships and led his teams to an unparalleled eighty-eight-game winning streak.

One simple discipline set Coach Wooden apart from every other coach before and after him: his unrelenting focus on the fundamentals. He believed this was the ultimate formula for success. No intricate plays. No hotshots or megastars. Just knowing and practicing the basics of the game over and over, until his players mastered them.

Whether you are an athlete, coach, or leader of a hospital fundraising office, it is important to remember that fundamentals should be the foundation of everything you do. Coach Wooden once said, "It's the little details that are vital. Little things make big things happen." I agree. If your hospital's fundraising office does not master the fundamentals, you will not achieve the results you seek. Focus on the fundamental elements of healthcare fundraising. It is human nature to want to skip past the fundamentals to find the next big thing that will achieve the best results in the shortest amount of time. However, a hospital fundraising office will get its most positive results if it simply focuses on mastering the fundamentals.

So, if basketball fundamentals are shoot, dribble, pass, and defend, then hospital fundraising fundamentals are thanking, asking, prospecting, and partnering. By far, the best way to maximize your hospital's fundraising is to concentrate on developing and improving these fundamental actions. And this chapter will provide four fundamentals for maximizing the value of your hospital's fundraising programs. These fundamentals include

- thanking philanthropic investors extraordinarily;
- asking philanthropic investors effectively;
- prospecting for new philanthropic investors thoroughly; and
- establishing beneficial community partnerships.

Thank Philanthropic Investors Extraordinarily

Hospital fundraising leaders know that success in the future of healthcare fundraising will be determined by how well we thank. While traditionally our profession has focused on perfecting the ask, hospitals must shift their attention to providing extraordinary displays of gratitude to their philanthropic investors. It is no longer enough to simply do good work, you must ensure that your hospital's positive impact is articulated clearly and powerfully to the community, and is directly connected to the philanthropic investment of individuals or organizations. Most philanthropic investors today will tell you that how they judge your hospital's fundraising program is just as much about how well they were thanked, and results were communicated as it was any other factor.

Good hospital fundraising offices have great systems and plans in place for soliciting philanthropic investments. However, best-practice hospitals compound those with extraordinary systems and plans for thanking and communicating impact with philanthropic investors in ways that ensure sustained support.

Thanking extraordinarily means being effective at the transactional practices of fundraising, such as sending thank-you notes quickly, verifying accuracy, sharing your hospital's plans for their investments, using a real signature, adding personal notes to letters, including cumulative philanthropy data, and making it clear if the letter also functions as a tax receipt. But it also means being very effective at the extraordinary elements too. Employ diverse, personalized expressions of appreciativeness and provide a gratitude experience that is memorable, valuable, and enjoyable. This includes using recognition and naming opportunities to increase philanthropic investor retention while also expressing to the community the transformative impact of philanthropy at your hospital. The ultimate goal of this extraordinary thanking is to provide an immersive experience to each philanthropic investor that inspires them to even greater levels of personal involvement and investment in your hospital.

To show your hospital's extraordinary gratitude, here are a few practical suggestions:

- Thank with public recognition and acknowledgment
- Thank with planned communications
- Thank by thoughtfully responding to questions
- Thank by using affinity-specific recognition societies
- Thank by helping to navigate your hospital and programs
- Thank with a focus on retention

Thank with Public Recognition and Acknowledgment

Using permanent commemorative displays, directory walls, and plaques can be powerful motivators. Be cost conscious, but remember that a well-designed recognition program serves for more than expressing gratitude to existing supports, it brings awareness to the community of more opportunities to get involved with philanthropy at your hospital.

Thank with Planned Communications

Create dynamic communications that are both investor-driven and story-focused to amplify the impact of your thanking and always provide timely, accurate documentation of philanthropic investments. A hospital fundraising office should focus on timely communications including receipts, recognition letters, impact reports, and annual report publications. Your hospital can communicate gratitude by sending a simple yet heartfelt thank-you card, providing recognition in a hospital publication, annual philanthropy report, or commemorative brochure.

Clear communication is essential in all relationships, and your philanthropic investors are no exception. Planned thank-you communications should help illuminate a shared sense of purpose, reiterate relevancy, and validate philanthropic investors' beliefs. Keep your fundraising communications interesting, informative, enjoyable, and not tiresome. The key is to provide high-value information, maintaining simplicity and clearly articulating the impact of philanthropic investment. Providing these well-conceived communications will create significant incentives for additional philanthropic investment as well.

Thank by Proactively Responding to Questions

Proactively answer philanthropic investors' questions: What's in it for me? Why does my contribution matter? Are my philanthropic goals aligned with hospital leadership's? What impact will my investment make? Will this hospital put my philanthropic priorities first or is this contribution process about them? Every question is an opportunity to strengthen your relationship with philanthropic investors and their understanding of their impact on your hospital.

Thank by Using Recognition Societies

Recognition societies offer a range of benefits that serve to both recognize the philanthropic investor for their philanthropy and continue cultivating them for future investments.

Recognition societies should be formed with set philanthropy requirements. These levels will provide meaningful recognition for philanthropic investors among their peers and the community, and thus can serve as powerful tools to inspire higher levels of philanthropic investment. Make your hospital's philanthropy levels sufficiently broad that they comprise a large group of philanthropic investors, but small enough that they maintain a sense of exclusivity. And be sure to integrate meaning in the naming of your societies. Best-practice hospitals use names that relate to their mission (e.g., founding date, retired admired physician, hospital building name, etc.) to provide a constant reminder of the group's shared purpose.

A hospital fundraising office should be creative about what you offer as benefits for philanthropy society members. Philanthropy societies also offer benefits like invitations to exclusive events, level-only newsletters, magazines, and reports, special lapel pins or buttons, and unique recognition in the annual report, on the website, etc.

Consistently encourage philanthropic investors to stretch their investments to reach the next society level. But remember that ultimately these societies exist to assist in delivering an extraordinary thank you to your philanthropic investors.

Thank by Helping to Navigate Your Hospital and Programs

Best-practice hospital fundraising offices help philanthropic investors navigate their healthcare system. There is nothing more important or personal than an individual's health, so when a philanthropic investor has a question about accessing care at your hospital, it is crucial they feel confident that you and the fundraising office will be able to help provide information and guidance.

Best-practice hospital fundraising offices facilitate medical appointments, offer support, and help guide them through their healthcare system. These fundraising offices provide solutions whenever possible and help their philanthropic investors coordinate their care with their entire healthcare team, including physicians, specialists, patient support systems, and community resources.

Thank with a Focus on Retention

Poor retention can cost a hospital's fundraising office substantial resources and significantly reduce the overall impact of philanthropic investment. And poor thanking practices are a driving force behind the poor philanthropic investor retention rates frequently achieved by hospitals. These low retention rates remind us again why thanking philanthropic investors extraordinarily is just as important as asking; it prompts repeated philanthropic investment, without which your fundraising operations are simply unsustainable.

When your hospital retains philanthropic investors, they will help to expand your reach and often will assist in attracting new investors. And when philanthropic investors are thanked extraordinarily, and their impact is articulated clearly and often, you can be sure they will relay their philanthropy experience to the community and become powerful promoters for your hospital.

And from a strategic planning standpoint, invest more staff and resources in retention of philanthropic investors. Understand the math; it's much more cost-effective to retain current philanthropic investors than it is to attract new ones. So, while many hospital fundraising offices continually seek to add solicitation officers, always assess the value of hiring staff dedicated to thanking philanthropic investors and ensuring excellent stewardship. Doing this will help retain philanthropic investors, increase their lifetime philanthropy to your hospital, and ultimately lower the overall costs of your fundraising operations.

> **important**
> Philanthropic investors value your hospital's work and want to help you change the world. They invest in the work they expect your hospital to accomplish. They want results. These practical suggestions and other ways of thanking philanthropic investors extraordinarily will be reviewed in **Chapter Four** as I address the importance of advancing and investing heavily in the philanthropy experience to keep your hospital investors happy and ensure that they receive the best stewardship possible.

Ask Philanthropic Investors Effectively

There is a well-known story about Henry Ford and his insurance salesman friend. Ford's friend tried to win a piece of Ford's sizeable insurance business for a long time only to learn one day that Ford had awarded the business to someone else. When the friend asked why, Ford responded, "You never asked."

Jack Canfield, a success coach, inspirational speaker, and creator of the *Chicken Soup for the Soul* series of books, has spent his life studying and reporting on what makes successful people different. In his book, *The Success Principles: How to Get From Where You Are to Where You Want to Be*, he outlines sixty-four principles for success. Principle seventeen is "Ask! Ask! Ask!" Canfield argues that asking is the world's most powerful and neglected secret to both success and happiness. He says that success requires taking the risk to ask for whatever you need and want. If someone says no, you are no worse off. But, if someone says yes, you are a lot better off.

In healthcare philanthropy, asking is such a critical part of effective fundraising, and yet even many seasoned fundraisers struggle with it. No matter how good a listener you are, how well you cultivate a relationship or use moves management, how well you pose questions, and how persistently you pursue a philanthropic investment, if you do not ask for an investment, you probably will not get it. To maximize the value of your hospital's fundraising program, you must focus on this most fundamental fundraising practice: being effective at asking. Make your needs, philanthropic priorities, and ask clear. Be concise and make it easy for philanthropic investors to say "yes." Finally, when you ask for anything, give a deadline if possible to create an understanding of the urgency of philanthropy.

Your hospital fundraising office needs to

- skillfully ask your hospital's top potential philanthropic investors;
- actively ask for planned philanthropy;
- resourcefully ask your hospital employees; and
- creatively ask, using modern communications.

Skillfully Ask Your Hospital's Top Potential Philanthropic Investors

Concentrate on your hospital's top potential philanthropic investors. One fundraising fundamental is to recognize that it is not about getting more prospective philanthropic investors, it is about focusing on the right prospective philanthropic investors.

Every successful, best-practice hospital fundraising office discovers that some philanthropic investors are more valuable than others. This can be for a range of reasons, from their financial capacity to the strength of their connection to your hospital's mission. Best-practice hospitals successfully prioritize soliciting the most valuable philanthropic investors.

> **Form a Principal Prospect Asking Team**
>
> Best-practice hospitals form a principal prospect team to focus on philanthropic investors who have the capacity and affinity to make big, transformational investments. These teams, often led by a principal relationship manager, provide ongoing, high-touch interaction with the hospital and its senior leadership. The team is highly focused on building relationships and connections with the highest potential philanthropic investors. They manage, facilitate, and further the cultivation and solicitation of a portfolio or high-capacity individuals capable of making lifetime commitments of seven to eight figure philanthropic investments. They develop linkages, passions, interests, and strategies with hospital priorities. They go above and beyond what is expected and look for opportunities to woo these individuals and build long-term loyalty. They urge the formation of informed, long-range strategies. They encourage philanthropic investors with extraordinary resources to make an extraordinary impact.
>
> 👍 practical tip

So, define exactly who the most valuable prospects are and spend time, almost every day, working to build those relationships. Manage your hospital's "moves" on cultivation toward a solicitation. For these unique relationships, it is important to build close personal relationships, keep in frequent touch, identify and resolve any issues or challenges they have quickly, and underpromise and over deliver, but make sure you always live up to expectations.

Actively Ask for Planned Philanthropy

Planned philanthropy, also known as planned giving, is becoming one of the most important, fundamental tools of hospital fundraising. This is because planned philanthropy focuses on a person's assets, which typically composes the bulk of a person's net worth. It is also because large generations of Americans, the baby boomers, are entering or have already reached retirement, have many medical needs, and frequently use your hospital, thus elevating the importance and value of planned philanthropy. It is time to market planned philanthropy opportunities more clearly and effectively. And it is time to establish a planned philanthropy strategy that offers your hospital's philanthropic investors even more ways to fulfill their philanthropic goals and touch the lives of others.

There is a well-known principle of medical diagnoses that is taught in medical schools called "Sutton's Law." It teaches that when diagnosing, one should first consider the obvious. The name of this principle was inspired by the notorious bank robber Willie Sutton, who supposedly replied to a reporter's inquiry as to why he robbed banks by saying, "because that's where the money is." Logic tells us as hospital fundraisers that we should also be following Sutton's Law. Why should we invest in planned philanthropy? Because that is where the obvious opportunity is for philanthropic investment. Over the next thirty to forty years, it is estimated that $30 trillion in financial and nonfinancial assets is expected to pass from the baby boomers to their heirs in the United States. Capitalizing on these intergenerational shifts in wealth will be critical. We must go where the money is.

Planned philanthropy is an effective process that determines which investment vehicle will provide the greatest philanthropic potential to both your philanthropic investors and your hospital. It is a process that allows philanthropic investors to achieve their financial objectives while also making larger philanthropic investments than otherwise possible. Planned philanthropy also expands a hospital's fundraising program by recognizing the viability of alternatives to outright philanthropic investments during uncertain economic times. There is considerable capacity for philanthropic investments crafted by way of bequests, trusts, life insurance, and other planned philanthropy vehicles. But the most important planned philanthropic investment is a simple bequest or revocable living trust. This type of philanthropy constitutes the largest volume of all the planned philanthropic investment vehicles.

Planned philanthropy ought to be included in all hospital communication. Consistent promotion and regular communication are essential. People are often unfamiliar with planned philanthropy and need to be educated that they can include your hospital in an estate plan.

Philanthropy experts Brian Sagrestano and Robert Wahlers have highlighted planned philanthropy strategies in several of their books. Specifically, I recommend *Getting Started in Charitable Gift Planning: Your Guide to Planned Giving* as a useful resource. In addition to their advice, focus on these fundamentals of building a robust planned philanthropy program:

- Set annual goals with specific targets such as number of visits, mailings, and most importantly, asks
- Initiate a recognition society for planned philanthropy investors
- Feature testimonials of planned philanthropy in hospital publications
- Create strong outreach to allied professionals (trust officers, financial planners, accountants, insurance consultants, attorneys, and investment and banking professionals)

Resourcefully Ask Your Hospital Employees

For many communities, the local hospital is often the biggest employer. And in most communities, the hospital is a source of comfort, healing, and pride. Capitalize on your hospital's status as a community pillar and engage your fellow hospital employees in philanthropy as an expression of pride and commitment.

To establish a vibrant employee philanthropy program, start by recruiting influential employees for leading the charge. Search for individuals who are widely valued and have dynamism, an optimistic spirit, resourcefulness, and passion for your hospital's mission. To inspire employee philanthropic

> **Involve Allied Professionals**
>
> Hospital fundraising offices must ally with professionals who can help advance planned philanthropy programs, such as trust officers, financial planners, accountants, insurance consultants, attorneys, and investment and banking professionals. These allied professionals prove invaluable in helping educate philanthropic investors, prospects, and volunteers.
>
> Getting allied professionals involved means making them aware of your fundraising case and providing them with general information about your hospital. It also means making them aware of opportunities and advances in legal, technical, or regulatory changes as they apply specifically to philanthropy planning. Best-practice hospital fundraising offices often call upon allied professionals to advise on planned philanthropy agreements, participate in seminars on estate and financial planning, and contribute articles to hospital fundraising publications about the tax aspects of planned philanthropic investments. However, the most valuable thing they can do is to promote your hospital fundraising office's planned philanthropy program and refer potential philanthropic investors to you.
>
> *practical tip*

investment, select employee leaders that are regarded as peers, not members of the hospital's senior management, with the aim of avoiding the conflict of managers "soliciting" their subordinates. Recruit a few select leaders and establish an employee fundraising committee with broad representation from numerous clinical departments and hospital areas. This volunteer committee of hospital employees will serve to spread the message to all areas of your hospital and engage each of your employees with philanthropy.

Additionally, make the employee philanthropy experience as easy and individualized as possible. Use tools like payroll deductions and specific areas of support to enable employees to easily make philanthropic investments to the programs for which they care about most. Remember, your hospital employees should receive the same consideration and attention as external philanthropic investors and the chance to align their personal philanthropy with their passions.

Set specific, ambitious, and achievable goals for your hospital employee philanthropy program and communicate frequently using hospital workplace means such as break-room tent cards, intranet sign-on screens, mailbox stuffers, posters, bulletin boards, newsletters, and email blasts. The objectives for your hospital employee philanthropy program should include

- ◆ 100 percent are aware of your employee philanthropy program;
- ◆ 100 percent are asked;
- ◆ 100 percent receive a follow-up to the ask; and
- ◆ 100 percent get an individualized thank you for participating.

It is particularly critical to thank hospital employees that participate as philanthropic investors when building an employee philanthropy program. Use premiums such as logo wear, t-shirts, tchotchkes, and pins to encourage involvement in philanthropy and link hospital employee philanthropy to fun and visible events such as a lunchtime picnic. Schedule incentives to be rewarded to all hospital employees when the philanthropy goal is reached.

Examples of hospital philanthropy participation incentives can range from paid days off, extra time for lunch or meal breaks, passes for dress-down or casual dress days, leave work early passes, and free pizza, ice cream, or coffee gatherings. And finally, recognize the generosity of employee philanthropic investors on listings in the hospital and in annual publications. All these activities will serve to communicate and publicize philanthropy and build excitement and momentum.

And remember to appreciate that hospital employee philanthropic investment makes a huge difference to outside funders. When external philanthropists see hospital employees step up in support of your hospital, it signals to the outside world that your hospital is a place worthy of philanthropic investment and that employees truly care about the mission. Participation rates in employee philanthropy programs by those who have an internal view of the hospital can make a strong impression on foundations, corporations, and individual philanthropy prospects.

Creatively Ask Using Modern Communications

Utilize the power of peer-to-peer asking to raise new philanthropic investment for your hospital. The expression "people give to people" means that philanthropic investors contribute to a need because they connect both with the solicitor and with the grateful patients whose lives will be enhanced by their investment.

Grow your social media presence and awareness of your cause by running a peer-to-peer fundraising campaign and capitalizing on digital networking opportunities. As more and more philanthropic investors receive communications and connect with your hospital via their smartphones, make sure everything you send out is "mobile-friendly."

Just as e-commerce grows, mobile philanthropic investing will continue to increase and be relied upon by philanthropic investors. Provide valuable and shareable content on social media and display opportunities to make philanthropic investments prominently on your hospital's website and social media.

Prospect for New Philanthropic Investors Thoroughly

Advancing technology and community connectedness mean we have more information about philanthropic investors available to us than ever before. How your hospital uses all this information and data will be critical to its fundraising success. Therefore, having robust systems for prospecting philanthropic investors is essential. Thoroughly prospecting philanthropic investors necessitates prospecting the wealthiest individuals within your community and prospecting for gratitude among your hospital's patients.

Prospect the Wealthiest Individuals Within Your Community

Targeting the right group of prospective philanthropic investors is critical. Focus your attention on the wealthiest people in your community to position your hospital for high return-on-investment (ROI) fundraising activity.

First, expand your prospect research and obtain information about philanthropic investors' interests and capabilities. This will help you to find new high-capacity philanthropic investors with an affinity for your hospital's mission. Start with individuals affiliated with your hospital, such as patients and vendors, past philanthropic investors, volunteers, and staff, and research their wealth. And, if possible, utilize data-screening services to verify and gather additional information.

But also appreciate, especially if your fundraising office has more limited resources, that a great deal of information can be found publicly. Home and business addresses, basic biographical information, degrees earned, and work history are all found with regular online searches of public sources. Being persistent with internet searching and using sources like LinkedIn or an employer's website can uncover additional biographical information. Additional basic information, including philanthropic investments made to other organizations, political candidate or party contributions, real estate holdings, and family foundation assets, can be found online. You can gain access to salary information for some professions like public university hospital leaders or professors, and the highest paid employees in a nonprofit organization. And because they are reported to the Securities and Exchange Commission, you can review publicly traded stock holdings and compensation of some corporate leaders.

If your hospital has access to and utilizes wealth screening software, remember results are not always entirely accurate, primarily because some information cannot be found publicly even with these screening services. Finding personal bank account or trust information is not possible. Additionally, compensation or stock holdings for any employee of a private company is rarely publicly available, unless it was reported in a news source. It is also very unlikely to find an individual's net worth, except for those estimates reported in *Forbes* or another news source.

Think hard about identifying the philanthropic investors most likely to contribute to your hospital. Make sure your hospital maintains a quality, targeted prospect list and concentrates on it. While there is much information not publicly available, remember to skillfully use the information you are able to gather to prospect for high-capacity philanthropic investors.

Professional prospect research leader Meredith Hancks has authored many books on the value of strategic prospect research. I would highly recommend her books, especially, *Getting Started in Prospect Research: What You Need to Know to Find Who You Need to Find* as an additional resource to help you enhance your prospecting for new philanthropic investors.

Prospect for Gratitude Among Your Hospital's Patients

Grateful patients are a primary target for philanthropic investment in most hospitals. While grateful patient philanthropic investment does hold more potential for some hospitals than others (i.e., hospitals that primarily serve patients with limited income and assets), remember that in addition to substantial philanthropic investments, you are prospecting for powerful testimonials for communicating value to your community.

Foster a Culture That Values Privacy

Your hospital fundraising office has the important responsibility of protecting the sensitive personal, financial, and personally identifiable protected health information (PHI) of your philanthropic investors. Protecting your philanthropic investor's private information against mishandling needs to be a top priority. It is not only good practice, in many cases, but it is also the law. So, make an extra effort to value, respect, and protect privacy by placing a high value on safeguarding the confidentiality and security of information. Breaches of privacy, confidentiality, or disclosure of personally identifiable protected health information may cause harm and result in embarrassment, bias, and discrimination. So, do everything you can to keep private information safe and to foster a culture that values privacy. This can include developing and posting a policy describing your current privacy practices fully and exactly as it relates to hospital fundraising.

Always be compliant with the Health Insurance Portability and Accountability Act (HIPAA) to foster a culture that values privacy. The act established national standards to protect individuals' medical records, created rules safeguarding the confidentiality and security of healthcare information, and set limits on information usage without patient consent, including uses for fundraising. The act was updated in 2013, clarifying the regulations fundraisers must respect to comply with the statute. Since 2013, hospital fundraising offices have had a greater ability to use PHI for fundraising purposes, to target their fundraising based on the nature of the services a patient received or the identity of a physician, and to engage physicians in the process of patient philanthropy.

> **important**
> Consult qualified legal counsel regarding how HIPPA may or may not affect your specific situation and refer to the Association for Healthcare Philanthropy or the Department of Health and Human Services for more information about HIPPA and its applicability.

It is important to protect privacy and health information. Take it seriously. Here are a few things your hospital fundraising office should do:

- Develop recurring privacy and HIPAA training. Privacy and HIPAA training should be a key component in your hospital fundraising office's onboarding process. Integrate confidentiality and HIPAA training through lectures, online training, and as part of your hospital fundraising office employee handbook.

- Have a database security professional monitor your hospital fundraising office activity regularly to ensure that all information remains safe. And limit hospital fundraising office staff access to patient data. Password-protect office computers to limit the number of people who have access to hospital patient records and specific sensitive financial data. And, create a standardized exit process and change passwords when staff members leave to ensure they don't take any confidential material with them.

- Offer straightforward and obvious opportunities to opt out. Your hospital's fundraising communications and the opt-out must be clear and conspicuous, explaining how PHI may be used. Opt-outs can be campaign-specific or for all future fundraising communications and do not lapse, even if a new philanthropic investment is made.

- Finally, even though you have put systems in place to ensure the highest level of privacy, be proactive and devise a response plan in the event confidential or protected health information disclosure violation occur. Plan for specific situations and address how you will assess damage or risk. Include steps to secure the information or remedy the situation.

Establishing Beneficial Community Partnerships

Establishing strong, beneficial community partnerships for your hospital requires

- securing the involvement of strong community volunteer leaders;
- maintaining connections with your hospital's clinicians;
- earning your clinicians' trust; and
- forming robust partnerships with corporations and foundations.

Securing the Involvement of Strong Community Volunteer Leaders

Volunteers are extremely helpful for expanding the reach and capabilities of your hospital's fundraising office. And the more connected to your hospital's mission and vision that your volunteers feel, the more likely they are to take the initiative and engage philanthropic investors. The involvement of strong community volunteers will

- ◆ help mobilize community resources and expand capacity;
- ◆ enhance your hospital's general profile; and
- ◆ attract even more volunteers and greater fundraising results.

Building a high-performing governing board with a commitment to and competence in philanthropy will provide the leadership necessary for sustainable fundraising success. A high-performing governing board will

- ◆ recognize its responsibility to drive excellent fundraising results;
- ◆ conduct substantive discussions of key issues affecting fundraising;
- ◆ make key strategic decisions to guide fundraising management;
- ◆ partner with the CEO or fundraising leaders to provide insight, advice, and support on key decisions; and
- ◆ carry out annual self-assessments and act on them.

Developing a high-performance board is an ongoing activity and a process of constant improvement. Hospital leaders must continually return to the same fundamental questions regarding purpose, resources allocation, and effectiveness to ensure maximization of the board's potential.

Maintaining Connections with Your Hospital's Clinicians

Your clinicians have an unparalleled role in engaging grateful patients with the life of your hospital. These clinicians are well-positioned to maximize grateful patient fundraising by sharing their powerful perspective on how philanthropic investment in your hospital is truly distinctive. And after philanthropic investments are secured and utilized, clinicians are in the best position to show direct appreciation and thank philanthropic investors for their generosity.

To build a tradition of rewarding clinician engagement with philanthropy, identify a select group of physician and nurse leaders and introduce them to the culture and fundamental characteristics of your fundraising program. Provide them with resources and training to strategically engage grateful patients in a manner that is consistent with their expectations of privacy and the sanctity of the clinician-patient relationship. As your clinicians become more familiar and comfortable with philanthropy, involve them on fundraising boards and in other fundraising activities.

Earning Your Clinicians' Trust

Do your clinicians trust you? Hospital fundraising offices with great clinician relationships are able to grow their fundraising tremendously. Your hospital fundraisers must be good at what they do but having a truly successful grateful patient program is based on one simple concept: trust. Because patients develop deep affinities for your hospital through their clinicians, the introductions, endorsements, and referrals that only clinicians can provide are critical to building strong relationships and achieving greater philanthropic investments for your hospital.

To maximize the potential of this partnership, there must be trust. Clinicians must trust that fundraisers are capable and that the fundraising process will produce results that positively impact their work. To help hospital fundraising professionals attain this essential trust transfer, I have identified six elements impacting clinician willingness to fundraise:

1. Clinicians always make their patients the top concern. They are not aware of all that your fundraising office does, so communicate the benefits you provide. How can you make their patient's lives easier or better? Real patient stories make excellent subject matter.

2. Clinicians are result-focused in their work. They want to see patients become healthier and they strive for positive outcomes. They will also expect your hospital fundraising office to prove results in your work. This requires establishing goals, communicating progress, and celebrating achievements regularly.

3. Clinicians have demanding time constraints, just like you. Make a special effort to accommodate their demanding schedules. Let them know when your fundraising office is engaging their patients and that the fundraising office will continue to communicate your interactions. Always keep them in the know and informed.

4. Clinicians know it is all about relationships. Just like you, clinicians engage with people they like, feel are competent,

and believe are successful. Be transparent and patient, provide resources, and set realistic goals and meet them to build rapport and trust. Clinicians will refer grateful patients with confidence when there is a strong and reliable relationship in place.

5. Clinicians tend to be risk averse. Reassure them that your fundraising office will protect them and their patient's personal information. With trust, you will have engaged clinical partners to work with you. Without trust, your fundraising office will not be successful.

6. Clinicians are motivated by respect and tradition. Leverage their desire for respect among peers and appeal to a sense of tradition to drive positive engagement with philanthropy.

When you think about how to better engage clinicians in philanthropy, make sure to recall these critical elements. And remember that the process of earning trust mirrors the process of sustaining it. Your hospital fundraising office must constantly work to provide support and assistance to clinicians partnering in philanthropy to maximize their potential to open doors to more and larger philanthropic investments.

Unfortunately, you likely have already realized many clinicians will not be interested in assisting. Don't be discouraged. Remember that those clinicians who are will be enormously valuable advocates for your hospital and phenomenal motivators for philanthropic investors.

In **Chapter Four** of this book, I will expand on clinician engagement in philanthropy and share more details regarding why it is imperative to invest in the process of making them key advocates in motivating grateful patients to become philanthropic investors.

Forming Robust Partnerships with Corporations and Foundations

Many of your community's valuable organizations have a vested interest in securing the future health of the area. Look for these organizations, predominately corporations and foundations, and partner with them to achieve their philanthropic goals through philanthropy to your hospital.

Foundations: For hospitals with innovative health programs, foundations remain important prospective philanthropic investors. Keys to successfully soliciting foundation funding are to identify and communicate hospital projects that align with the foundation's philanthropy priorities and to utilize the networks of hospital leadership and clinicians to gain advocates within the targeted foundation.

Corporations: Implement a corporate philanthropy program with clearly identified opportunities for publicly recognized impact. Corporations generally want added motivation, such as publicity, exposure, or other recognition. Knowing this, provide them with the option to become sponsors of events or other programs. Be sure to demonstrate how a relationship with your hospital is mutually beneficial and describe how you can leverage your hospital's reach and promote their contributions to the local community.

Linda Lysakowski has provided very practical advice on how to succeed in developing and implementing long-term partnerships with corporations and businesses. In particular, Linda's book, *Raise More Money from Your Business Community: A Practical Guide to Tapping Into Corporate Charitable Giving* is an excellent resource for expanded information on this important topic.

To Recap

The best way to maximize your hospital's fundraising is to

- ◆ thank philanthropic investors extraordinarily;
- ◆ ask philanthropic investors effectively;
- ◆ prospect for new philanthropic investors thoroughly; and
- ◆ establish beneficial community partnerships.

Chapter Three

Measuring the Value of Your Fundraising to Ensure High Performance and Effectiveness

IN THIS CHAPTER

- Utilize classic fundraising performance metrics
- Observe engagement and activity metrics
- Monitor philanthropic investment level metrics
- Pursue unique performance metrics

Prominent business management thinker Peter Drucker is remembered by many for popularizing the saying "You can't manage what you can't measure." And as the American healthcare system has transitioned from a fee-for-service to a value-based model, the demand for performance metrics has never been greater. Data on medical complications, hospital-acquired infections, and readmissions is now helping to drive improvements in community health and healthcare delivery nationwide. And analytics tools are allowing for more sophisticated tracking and measurement. High-quality metrics can now inform hospitals when to change ways or reallocate resources or if one of their approaches, methods, or channels is struggling or doing significantly better than expected.

And just as physicians, nurses, and administrators are using data and metrics to lower costs and improve patient experiences, hospital fundraising offices must harness these tools to measure value and improve performance. But effectively measuring the value of any hospital fundraising office is no small task. There must be a holistic performance measurement approach, diligent tracking of resource allocation, detailed planning and reporting, and the integration of analytics directly into reporting tools and decision processes. After all, how can you know what works unless you measure your results and track them over time?

But before best-practice hospital fundraising offices begin to measure value, they first develop an appreciation for the impact of the various measurement systems and tools available. They do this because they know fundraising measurement systems strongly affect the behavior of fundraisers, managers, processors, and volunteer leaders—all of whom are essential to a high-performing fundraising office. They know that certain methods of measuring fundraising value can be detrimental to individual fundraising results and a hospital fundraising team's overall effectiveness. And finally, they know that there is no "one-size-fits-all" value measurement and that you will likely need to blend and prioritize different metrics to find a system that fits the unique direction of your hospital.

As you begin to assess how to best measure the value of your fundraising office, determine what questions you seek to have answered by your value measurements. Do you want to know the efficiency of your hospital's fundraising operations? Do you want to know how much your hospital spends for every dollar raised? Maybe you want to be able to compare the return on investment for different fundraising revenue streams or against peer hospitals. Also, be mindful that your value measurements are not only useful to the fundraising office and hospital leaders; these tools are also increasingly being used by prospective philanthropic investors to determine the organizations and causes most capable of creating positive impact from their contribution. So, whatever questions you and your philanthropic investors seek to have answered should guide how you develop your hospital's value

> **What Are KPIs?**
>
> Key performance indicators are a group of measurable values that show how effective you are at achieving key performance objectives. They are used to evaluate success at reaching specific goals and targets. They are selected based on the performance improvements you are looking to achieve and often established because of a situation and part of your fundraising operation needing attention. They are best tracked using a simple dashboard or routine printed account.
>
> **principle**

measurement system and form the key performance indicators (KPIs) that express the overall value of philanthropy.

Learn where you are coming from, where you currently stand, and where you are heading by concentrating on time. The value of measuring and recording a hospital's fundraising performance increases exponentially over time. Monthly metric dashboards and reports illustrate short-term changes and trends. Metrics over several years can draw attention to long-term trends. Showcase your performance year on year on the same activities to help you understand whether your output has increased or diminished.

Several means can be used to measure the effectiveness of your hospital fundraising, expose strengths and challenges, and reveal opportunities to make a greater impact. The following four categories encapsulate the major facets of fundraising value measurement:

- Utilizing classic fundraising performance metrics
- Observing engagement and activity metrics
- Monitoring philanthropic investment level metrics
- Pursuing unique performance metrics

Utilize Classic Fundraising Performance Metrics

Just as there are an overwhelmingly large number and variety of metrics that can be used to evaluate the success of your hospital's clinical programs, there are also many methods for measuring a hospital fundraising office's performance. Fortunately, certain classic metrics are commonly used to form the basis for value measurement as well as to inform strategic decision-making, planning, activities, and deployment of resources.

Total Philanthropic Investments Secured

The total philanthropic investments secured is calculated by summing the total number of philanthropic investments finalized in a given period. For example: how many philanthropic investments did your hospital secure through the month? The quarter? The year? It is useful because it provides a high-level overview of your fundraising office's overall and program-level performance. It is an incredibly simple and standard measurement for assessing fundraising performance. It also provides you with a sense of the size of your philanthropic community. Best-practice hospitals also often separate the philanthropic investments by types, such as major, planned, special-level, annual fund, and online to further assess value and effectiveness.

Total Fundraising Net

Total fundraising net is calculated by subtracting your total fundraising expenses from your total amount raised. It measures the amount that is left after deducting all fundraising and administrative expenses from the total fundraising revenue and reveals the amount of money available to you to spend on your hospital's mission as a result of its fundraising efforts. For example, if your hospital raised $2,000,000 and spent $500,000 on operating expenses to do it, your hospital fundraising office's total fundraising net is $1,500,000 ($2,000,000 − $500,000 = $1,500,000).

Cost per Dollar Raised

Cost per dollar raised (CPDR) is calculated by dividing the total fundraising expenses by the total fundraising net. It measures how much it costs to raise money. It is useful because it is an uncomplicated measure of efficiency and enables your fundraising office to quickly determine how much money your hospital spends to raise a single dollar. It is often a key performance indicator and a straightforward way to see if your hospital was successful or unsuccessful at raising philanthropic investment.

Best-practice hospital fundraising offices conventionally establish overall CPDR goals as well as goals for specific initiatives and individual fundraisers. By and large, hospital fundraising offices seek a lower cost of fundraising, indicating they are investing efficiently in fundraising. The industry average for CPDR is between twenty-five and thirty-five cents spent for every dollar raised. Though, there are quite a few variables, such as your hospital fundraising office's age or maturity of fundraising programs, your pool of affluent individual prospects, the size of your fundraising staff, and the location of your hospital.

Retention Rate of Philanthropic Investors

The retention rate of philanthropic investors (RRPI) is calculated by first determining the number of philanthropic investors to your hospital in one year (Year One), and the number of philanthropic investors from that same pool who also made an investment in the subsequent year (Year Two). Then, divide Year Two by Year One. It measures how many philanthropic investors your fundraising office retains on a year-over-year basis. It is useful because it assesses the strengths and weaknesses of your retention practices. It tests your acknowledgment processes, your follow-up, and your communications with philanthropic investors. Low retention rates among certain philanthropic investor segments can help to inform your fundraising office of additional stewardship needs. Conversely, high retention rates can help illuminate particularly successful stewardship activities that can be implemented across a larger group.

A white paper published in 2013 by Blackbaud, a supplier of software and services for nonprofit organizations, reported that overall repeat philanthropic investor retention rates fluctuated between 53 percent and 70 percent depending on the nonprofit category. Retention rates for first-timers fell to 35 percent, and even as low as 20 percent in some categories. So, it is feasible your hospital could be losing, on average, almost one of every two philanthropic investors every year.

Hospital fundraising offices often put much more importance on acquisition than retention, looking to increase their dollars raised by looking "out there" for a quick solution and pouring a large chunk of their fundraising communication's budgets into acquisition mailings or grateful patient referral programs. However, research shows that this method may not necessarily be the best route to take for improving dollars raised and ROI. In fact, the numbers indicate quite the opposite. Acquiring new philanthropic investors can be expensive, and retention is proven to be more cost-effective. Before looking outside to bring in new philanthropic investors, hospital fundraising offices should turn their attention to the philanthropic investors who are already within their grasp and find ways to generate more and increased investment from them by turning them into repeat investors who are loyal to your programs. Prioritizing the use of RRPI as a measurement tool can help build a culture that seeks to retain before it acquires.

Increasing your base of philanthropic investors is the fastest way to grow your dollars raised and the most obvious way to reach short-term revenue goals. You expand your philanthropic investor numbers by way of acquisition, but you keep your philanthropic investor pool through retention. Resources are finite and when measuring your output you should be able to quantify what percentage of time and effort was put toward new philanthropic investors vs. those you already have. Your acquisition and retention rates should be improving simultaneously. And RRPI, when used to draw actionable plans for improved philanthropic investor stewardship, can help your fundraising office keep your current philanthropic investors interested and engaged.

Growth Rate of Philanthropic Investors

Growth rate of philanthropic investors (GRPI) is calculated by subtracting year one philanthropic investors from year two philanthropic investors first, then dividing Year One Philanthropic Investors and multiply by one hundred. It is a simple measurement that shows you by what percentage your philanthropic investor pool grows each year. It is useful because it helps to ensure that you're paying attention to your overall performance, not simply satisfying current philanthropic investors or acquiring new. While retaining philanthropic investors should be your fundraising office's top priority, acquiring new philanthropic investors and growing your base is certainly critical to long-term success.

Observing Engagement and Activity Metrics

To achieve specific fundraising results, you must perform specific activities. Through these metrics, you can guide your hospital fundraising team to the right activities that will result in securing more philanthropic investments. These metrics help your team focus on engagement and the activities that are important. And they provide you with visibility into how your team is performing against select activity goals. When you observe activity falling behind, you can course-correct by drilling into the data and seeing who or what area needs support, help, or coaching around what activities. Observing engagement and activity metrics turns reactive management into proactive leadership.

Contact Frequency with Philanthropic Investors

Contact frequency with philanthropic investors (CFPI) is calculated by tracking a targeted number of "moves" or "touches" per year to prospective philanthropic investors. It measures the various types of productive contact philanthropic investors have with your fundraising office and includes phone calls, visits, meetings, invitations, emails, etc. It is useful because it keeps records of all philanthropic investor-staff interactions in your database. This calculation is oftentimes referred to as tracking "moves management." "Moves management," a concept developed by David Dunlop, a philanthropy professional at Cornell University, describes the idea that frequent and strategic contacts with people can change their attitudes toward philanthropy. "Moves" are any actions that your hospital fundraising office takes to move someone from cultivation to solicitation. The objectives of a moves management process are to identify prospective philanthropic investors, segment based on their potential value and profile, nurture and cultivate, and analyze for improvements.

Percentage of Prospects in Each Stage of the Pipeline

The percentage of prospects in each stage of the pipeline is calculated by counting the total number of philanthropic investors in your pipeline, including only those with top capacity. During your work, prospects will travel or "move" through four stages in your pipeline: identification, cultivation, solicitation, and stewardship. This metric looks at the percentage of your prospective and current philanthropic investors in each of these four phases. Tracking percentages in the pipeline helps your hospital fundraising office with its efficiency and effectiveness, and knowing how many philanthropic investors you have in each stage tells you if you are moving investors along at the right rate and if you have any weaknesses by stage. It's a great metric for evaluating the overall fluidity of your hospital fundraising program.

Conversion Rate

Conversion rate is calculated by first starting with an "action" and a philanthropic investor list. The action could be anything from attending a golf outing event or ticketed gala to responding to a direct mail letter. Next, you divide the number of people who completed the action by the total number of people who were given the opportunity to do so. Then multiply the number by one hundred to get a percentage. For example, if your fundraising office pushes out an email requesting a thousand people to follow a link and make a philanthropic investment, and four hundred responded to the email by following the link and making a philanthropic investment, then your conversion rate for this goal is 40 percent. It is useful because it is the most objective method of evaluating the success of a given request for action.

Average Investment Size Per Individual Fundraiser

The average philanthropic investment size per individual fundraiser is calculated by taking the total revenue generated by a specific fundraiser during a specific time frame by the number of investments they received in that same period. It is a solid measure of an individual fundraiser's performance. However, it is wise to be prudent in applying this measurement alone to track performance, because in many instances closing major philanthropic investments can take upwards of twenty months.

Asks Made

The number of asks made is calculated by tracking the number of times your hospital fundraising office or a specific individual fundraiser explicitly asks for a philanthropic investment in a certain time. It encourages a focus on asking and negotiating final agreements. Best-practice hospital fundraising offices typically set monthly goals for asks made and are actively engaged with this metric. The metric is beneficial because it guarantees that ask frequency is a focus. As the saying goes, "if you are not asking you are not raising!"

Monitoring Philanthropic Investment Level Metrics

Monitoring philanthropic investment levels helps your hospital fundraising office to make informed decisions that drive strategy and ultimately helps you achieve better fundraising results. It helps you evaluate if you need to be asking your current philanthropic investors to increase their next investment, invest more often, or increase the size of a pledge that they have already made.

Average Philanthropic Investment Size

Average philanthropic investment size is calculated by taking the total amount of all philanthropic investments in your hospital over a specific time frame and dividing it by the total number of investments. It informs your hospital fundraising office on the typical size of investment you will receive from a philanthropic investor. It measures if investment sizes are decreasing, stagnating, or growing. It can be more sensitive to outlier investment sizes, so a longer time frame will give you a clearer picture. Advancing your philanthropic investors by asking them to increase their average investment size is important because it is the single easiest way to increase your annual fundraising revenue.

Pursuing Unique Performance Metrics

There are some performance metrics based on the unique conditions of the hospital fundraising industry, or activities they distinctively do, such as grateful-patient referrals, peer-to-peer event fundraising participation rates, percentages of online philanthropy, philanthropic investor transfers, and opt-out rates.

Grateful Patient Referrals

The grateful patient referral total is calculated by tracking the number of grateful patient referrals from referring clinicians. Your hospital's clinicians have the potential to serve as your best ally in promoting philanthropy. Their contact and interaction with patients and gratitude is unparalleled and, if tracked and managed, can lead to significant fundraising results. Tracking the number of grateful patient referrals, the referring clinicians, and conversion rate can help your hospital fundraising office to identify top clinician allies and to generate more and larger grateful patient philanthropic investments.

Peer-to-Peer Event Fundraising Participation Rate

Peer-to-peer fundraising is a method of fundraising that leverages your hospital's supporters to fundraise on your behalf. It is also known as social fundraising and/or team fundraising. Examples include milestone events, such anniversaries, birthdays, graduations, challenge events such as climbing an office tower staircase, swimming a local lake, or cutting off hair, and activities such as dance marathons, running events, biking tours, or walkathons for which participants fundraise in order to participate.

The peer-to-peer event fundraising participation rate is calculated by determining the total number of fundraising event participants that raise funds for an event or activity. For example, if your hospital hosts an event and a participant simply pays an entry fee, they are not a "fundraiser" for purposes of this metric. However, if, in addition to their entry fee, that same participant gathers pledges to support their ride, they are then a "fundraiser."

Event attendees who make philanthropic investments and double as fundraisers are unique assets and can help to rapidly grow your hospital's network of supporters. This metric is increasingly useful because peer-to-peer fundraising is growing in popularity. When establishing fundraising participation rate goals, also consider capturing other data, such as number of emails sent by participants, number of event philanthropic investments raised per participant, and amount raised per participant.

Percentage of Online Philanthropy

The percentage of online philanthropy is calculated by computing the percentage of philanthropic investments received online. Online philanthropy is the way of the future. Tracking the percentage of philanthropic investments received digitally is critical to forming a strategic and targeted digital engagement strategy. It will inform your hospital fundraising office on when to scale down outdated fundraising methods as well as which online philanthropy strategies are most successful.

Several best-practice hospital fundraising offices use additional advanced metrics, such as tracking which online traffic sources are driving the most philanthropic investments to their philanthropy website and the popular pages visited prior to a philanthropic investor visiting their hospital's online philanthropy page.

Philanthropic Investor Transfers

Philanthropic investor transfers are calculated by determining how well your fundraising office is transferring philanthropic investors from one program, typically annual philanthropy, into another program, typically major giving. It is useful because one of the key goals in any hospital fundraising office should be to transition philanthropic investors to higher and higher levels of investment. So, if you find your hospital fundraising office has struggling philanthropic investor transfers from one level to the next, this could be a sign that annual fund staff and major gift officers may need to focus on identifying and implementing new strategies to guide philanthropic investors to greater levels of support.

Opt-Out Rate

The opt-out rate is calculated by taking the number of patient opt-outs in a year and dividing by the number of patient records in a year. It measures the number of individuals that no longer wish to receive fundraising information from your fundraising office. A high opt-out rate could mean that your philanthropy culture is not established or understood or your nonprofit status and mission are not clear in your community. If possible, collecting why patients opt out of receiving fundraising materials can provide valuable information. Identifying the opt-out rate of fundraising is a good discipline and important because of HIPAA privacy regulations. Tracking helps you avoid violating patient wishes and privacy and makes sure your filters are set to avoid a breach situation.

Conclusion

Like any other business, your hospital fundraising office has a limited budget. There simply isn't an endless pool of funds to invest in promoting philanthropy. But developing the best systems and tools for measuring value in your fundraising office will help you invest in what works and will put your valuable fundraising budget toward effective strategies.

Your fundraising office's unique set of value measurements and KPIs will help you be selective, strategic, and smart in where you invest your operating dollars. They will help you to focus on shedding low return-on-investment activities and investing in value. And, they add an important layer of further knowledge and insight into your fundraising decision-making.

Ultimately, measuring value in your fundraising office should increase its value. Appreciate that the tools and systems reviewed here are just the beginning and that fundraising analytics tools are always evolving, just like healthcare. Stay in front of the newest value measurement tools and your hospital fundraising office will surely be poised for improvement and success.

To Recap

- ◆ Utilize classic fundraising performance metrics.
- ◆ Observe engagement and activity metrics.
- ◆ Monitor philanthropic investment level metrics.
- ◆ Pursue unique performance metrics.

Chapter Four

Investing in Value to Build an Amazing Organization

IN THIS CHAPTER

- Invest in the people most important to your success
- Invest in your philanthropy brand
- Invest in stewardship efforts
- Invest in strategic planning for fundraising

Investing your fundraising office's resources in creating value will help to significantly improve your hospital's philanthropic results. While many hospital leaders worry about spending too much on supporting their fundraising office, if your hospital is serious about expanding fundraising and achieving new heights, substantial investment is crucial.

Always remember that value is constantly evolving. Highly valued concepts from 10 years ago are now commonplace. And while a failure to evolve often results in a failure to retain philanthropic investors, if your fundraising office is constantly investing in creating value, you will both retain philanthropic investors and attract new ones. Therefore, it is necessary for even the highest functioning hospital fundraising offices to continually invest in creating value. To build up the value of your fundraising office, focus on these four key areas:

1. Invest in the people most important to your success
2. Invest in your philanthropy brand

3. Invest in stewardship efforts

4. Invest in strategic plan for fundraising

Invest in the People Most Important to Your Success

Invest in your people to get the best from your people. When people feel supported, they have the space to be creative and do their best work. It all starts with culture and values. And it starts with investing in the people most important to your success: your staff, your top hospital leadership, your hospital's clinicians, and your volunteer leaders.

Invest in Your Staff

Investment in staff must be a top priority of your hospital fundraising office. Areas of focus should include professional development for staff, training for volunteers, and access to the best resources to help increase team effectiveness. To guide investment in your fundraising staff, concentrate on these five actions:

- Recruit the best
- Improve training
- Reward success
- Develop culture
- Reward performance

Recruit the Best

Association for Healthcare Philanthropy research shows that the highest-performing hospital fundraising offices invest in acquiring larger staffs and raise almost thirty times more than those with smaller teams. View adding staff to a fundraising team as an investment made in revenue. Recognizing that this is an investment is a critical first step toward improving the value of your fundraising office.

Pay fundraisers better-than-average salaries and give raises for top performers. Devote a good chunk of money to hiring fundraisers who will focus on attracting big philanthropic investment, bequests, and other planned philanthropy, as the best-practice hospital fundraising offices do. Hire people who enjoy getting out of office because they will give more individual attention to prospects by conducting more face-to-face visits. Attract the best workers.

Improve Training

Provide proper training for all fundraising staff. Don't just "throw information at 'em" and hope some of it sticks. Consider training needs from a number of angles. Include hospital orientation, hospital service knowledge, healthcare knowledge, and fundraising training. Have ride-alongs or shadow experiences for newer fundraisers and incorporate active engagement exercises, repetition, and specific goal setting, as well as direct application and accountability for what's being learned.

Ask your top-producing philanthropy officers to help a junior philanthropy officer with a prospect or moves management challenge. Invest in training and educational opportunities because there is always new technology, new tools, new approaches, and new opportunities that you need to keep on top off. Set aside budget and training days or retreats in which you and your team can learn. Go to seminars and conferences that teach the essential skills and knowledge needed to do work more efficiently and smoothly. Reinforce the training and observe them in the field putting it to use.

And if financially viable, educate and develop your staff by attending an Association of Fundraising Professionals or Association for Healthcare Philanthropy conference or a local nonprofit educational event. These opportunities give employees more experience, confidence, and understanding of how to improve in their profession.

Develop Culture

Develop a philanthropy-focused fundraising culture and encourage collaboration and cooperation across the hospital fundraising office. Be focused on serving and promoting the best interests of the philanthropic investors first. Share information and discuss prospective philanthropic investors as a group. Talk about philanthropy failures or philanthropic investor relations challenges openly and without blame. Ask everyone on the team to weigh in on a particularly tough prospect or stewardship challenge. Have everyone in your organization involved and supportive of the fundraising process. Know that in bad cultures, fundraisers often get caught up in the role of philanthropic investor advocate because if they don't, no one else will. Also know that in bad cultures, demands on fundraising staff can be unrealistic, so they react by overpromising, which puts an unnecessary and unwanted burden on many.

But don't confuse a supportive culture as one lacking fierce competition. Top fundraising offices benefit from a little dose of positive peer pressure.

Appreciate that most top fundraisers respond well to some degree of positive competition. Be aware that friendly wagers can lift and motivate. Use public goals, closure rates, and other activity stats to drive fundraising staff to new levels of achievement.

Fight boredom and tedium, they are the enemy of progress. A dull atmosphere leads to disengagement and decreased productivity in everyone. Build a team and socialize, keep it fun. Improve morale by offering work-life balance through reduced or flexible work schedule programs and providing the flexibility to do some work remotely, it is becoming more commonplace. Pay for services that promote work-life balance. Offer other "perks" that promote health and correspondingly increase satisfaction and productivity, such as gym membership or fitness credit.

Reward Performance

When your staff achieves highly, praise them! Many top fundraisers love praise and thrive on it. Research suggests top performers are even willing to sacrifice incentive bonuses for public recognition. Make it a standard practice in your office to recognize positive people. Announce publicly when one of your fundraisers makes a particularly outstanding presentation, secures a difficult visit, assembles a proposal, pulls together a noteworthy solicitation team, makes notable achievements, and give this sincere praise in front of others.

And while you should praise staff publicly, it is best to provide corrections privately. Appreciate that most people are not motivated by negative feedback. Do not embarrass them, and be sure to close the door or go off-site when providing negative feedback. Don't think of correcting a fundraiser's performance or behavior as punitive. Instead, consider it a learning opportunity. Keep an open mind. Present issues in such a way that the fundraiser feels they can correct. Discuss weakness or errors in the context of, "I know you can and will do better."

Demonstrate interest in fundraisers' long-term development and create career growth experiences. Appreciate for some, the ultimate reward is an opportunity to get ahead in their careers. Offer incentives that help fundraisers develop skills to move to next level. Discuss goals and interests. And acknowledge the need for challenge, achievement, and professional growth. Provide opportunities for professional development through conferences, classes, or workshops. Offer leadership opportunities when possible, to help foster leadership growth and succession opportunities. And seek out natural strengths and determine if there is a project team or hospital committee that could use those skills.

If a hospital fundraiser is performing at a high level, find new and expanded ways to engage them in the hospital and decision-making process. Give them say in an important project or team that influences the direction of your hospital fundraising office. Ask for and incorporate their feedback in your business plans and ongoing projects. Let them voice their opinions on who to hire, where to expand next, and what projects to concentrate on. Be open to their new ideas and innovative approaches. And present these top performers with difficult challenges.

Recognize the motivating value of unraveling puzzles and obstacles. Give them the really difficult challenges and prospects. Confirm you have confidence in them. Allow them to directly observe outcomes that are a clear result of their effort. And ultimately, reward effective performance. Pay top performers more and give them bigger bonuses, if possible. Make strategic salary adjustments. Don't adhere to rigid rules. Vary the basis for the awards. Recognize several types of excellence. Offer rewards for all the areas that contribute to your fundraising office's success.

Invest in Your Relationship with Top Hospital Leadership

Since the Patient Protection and Affordable Care Act (ACA) was signed into law in 2010, the economic environment for healthcare has changed significantly. And with shifting national leadership after the 2016 presidential election, continued change is inevitable. Relationships between medical providers and hospitals will evolve. Technology will improve. And with these major changes, it's more important than ever to invest in your relationship with your top hospital leadership.

The strength and breadth of the relationships between your fundraising office and hospital leaders are essential to expanding your reach and increasing your philanthropic results. So, as a hospital fundraising leader, you must invest in these relationships and work hard to build alignment and trust. You need to cultivate trust by building a connection and rapport and showing your knowledge and business acumen, and consistently deliver results.

Remember that respect and relationships are built through personal connections, so you must invest ample time to develop comraderies with each hospital leader. Learn how your hospital CEO and leaders think and what matters to them. Solicit their perspectives on what they see as the hospital's key challenges, as well as their view of philanthropy's function and effectiveness. These conversations will help you learn more about your hospital and assist you in developing fundraising objectives and strategies.

When building relationships with top hospital leaders, be sure to establish clear expectations for philanthropic investment at your hospital. Provide frequent and regular communication and be transparent in your interactions. You must be open, frank, and honest in your communications. And always be brief and effective in communicating what is most important for them as executives to know and understand. Be respectful of their time. Provide solid financial advice as it relates to philanthropy and build trust with candor and facts. Speak with candor and substantiate positions with data and analysis. Present your results in simple and efficient ways. Being transparent in your interactions also means you challenge appropriately, are bold when it's important, and are helpful routinely.

Your executive colleagues will recognize the value of you being objective, focused, and occasionally critical. Share information, ideas, forward-looking options, and solutions. Be open, honest, and thick-skinned and, because it is healthcare, always be flexible and willing to make changes, sometimes hastily. Deliver on your commitments and ensure that you and your team are getting them done as promised.

With your CEO, especially, be their right hand and show them that you understand how he or she thinks about the critical hospital issues. Put yourself in their shoes and proactively help your CEO.

> **Accounting and Reporting**
>
> Your hospital fundraising office needs relevant information in real time concerning the performance of your resources and fundraising projects. Technology today can provide real-time statistics that give your hospital fundraising office immediate insight into how your resources and projects are functioning. This allows your hospital fundraising office to make immediate adjustments to resources or projects to improve performance and results. Increased interest and scrutiny into the nonprofit area means that record keeping is vital. Use up-to-date technology to capture the details of every interaction including the history of each and every contact, phone and email records, and, of course, financial data.
>
> **observation**

Understand the CEO's needs and desires and bring solutions and plans. Be a sounding board and advisor as it relates to philanthropic investors but also community relations. Find ways to make sure your personalities are compatible. If necessary, adapt your style just as you do for different prospective philanthropic investors. Get on the same page and develop a common vision for your hospital's fundraising office and its operating philosophy. And just like with philanthropic investors, listen well, offer counsel when the time is right, spend time talking about all aspects of philanthropy and people, not just dollars and cents, balance expressing your own view with helping the CEO formulate their view, and don't be afraid of tough conversations.

Make your CEO look good. Set your CEO up for success. Make the CEO's job as the hospital's top fundraiser easier. Raise your voice, no matter how prickly it might be for you. Build trust because it is central to any good, sustained relationship, personal or professional. As a CEO, you are privy to sensitive information from many sources. Never violate confidences, so talk over any rules that your CEO has about how information the two of you discuss can be shared, and with whom. And sometimes speak the tough truth. Let them know when they said or did something with a philanthropic investor that had an unenthusiastic, unhelpful, or negative impact. Dealing with potential issues on the front end helps remove ambiguity and speculation that could fuel destructive gossip.

Remember, you are a hospital executive first. This means developing a deep understanding of the hospital and healthcare industry. This also means understanding strategy, developing informed insights, having a holistic view of the hospital, and maintaining a balanced perspective. Don't just focus on philanthropy, focus on helping improve your entire hospital. And, drive focus and alignment. Develop a comprehensive view on mission, strategy, implementation. Focus on things that move the needle. To do this, you need to get to know your CEO, colleagues, and your team. Establish clear expectations. Deliver on your commitments. Demonstrate trust. Give the CEO and hospital leaders reason to have confidence in you. Show them that you are running the hospital fundraising office well. Communicate openly and honestly with them. Listen to them.

Invest in Your Connections with Clinicians

The late Victor Fazio, M.D. served as the Chairman of the Department of Colon and Rectal Surgery for thirty-eight years at the Cleveland Clinic. He was one of the highest-regarded colorectal surgeons in the world and truly a value-based caregiver. He was committed to perfection, professionalism, and integrity. And, his commitment to his patients was beyond compare. During my time as the Director of Development at the Cleveland Clinic's Digestive Disease Institute, I had the pleasure of raising philanthropic investment for Dr. Fazio's programs and he taught me how to build trust with clinicians, how to talk with clinical teams, medical staff, and specialty groups about grateful patient philanthropy, and why investing in your connections with clinicians was so valuable.

Year after year, grateful patients and their family members are consistently among the largest sources of philanthropic investment in healthcare. And relationships with these top philanthropic investors are almost always initiated by clinicians through both simple, routine encounters and life-altering experience. Because of this, top hospital fundraising offices invest substantially in engaging their clinicians as key advocates for philanthropy.

Investing in connecting clinicians with philanthropy requires an institution-wide commitment to recognizing patients with both a propensity and capacity to support the hospital, from the advocate who greets patients at the front desk to the physicians and nurses who provide them with care. To invest in your hospital's clinicians, focus on these five actions:

- ◆ Educating
- ◆ Communicating
- ◆ Engaging
- ◆ Trusting
- ◆ Tracking

Educating

Even amid their demanding schedules, it is important to work with clinicians to find the time to provide proper education on their role with philanthropy at your hospital. Arming your clinicians with easy-to-understand information about the function and impact of philanthropy at your hospital and how to connect grateful patients with the fundraising office is the critical first step.

In addition, you should provide your clinicians with simple, yet attractive takeaways that they can use to inform both themselves and their patients about philanthropy. Many clinicians also find it helpful to have sample language that depicts how to navigate conversations regarding philanthropy with patients. Above all else, clinicians will seek to protect their patient's privacy, so providing education about HIPAA regulations is important to ensuring their buy-in to the fundraising process. And be sure to always include the appropriate contact information to reach the hospital fundraising office.

As you work to educate your clinicians about partnering with philanthropy, your fundraising office's larger goal should be to develop a formalized program and structure for engaging clinicians. While constructing and executing a robust clinician engagement program may seem complex and demanding, remember that this investment will create significant increasing value for your hospital for years to come.

Communicating

When good communication is lacking, misunderstanding occurs. Be available to clinicians through dedicated time listening and communicating. Give clinicians a voice in philanthropy at your hospital. They will often have a unique and powerful perspective on projects and initiative that deserve philanthropic priority, so allow clinicians to provide input during decision-making processes. Make a true commitment to your clinicians and listen to their ideas, and you will uncover a great deal of information, problems, values, and opinions that should be used in philanthropic decision-making.

Make sure the clinicians understand the "ins and outs" of patient gratitude, your hospital's principal fundraising objectives, how philanthropy benefits their objectives, and overall institutional goals. Then communicate the variety of roles they can play in the philanthropy process. Include information about philanthropy and the hospital fundraising office in employee orientations, in physician and physician practice meetings, and hospital-wide meetings.

Engaging

Discover which clinicians you can build strong relationships with and engage them in the philanthropy program. Consider creating a Clinician Philanthropy Leadership Council to lead by example, meet regularly, guide the grateful patient program, help to enlist other, more reluctant members of the staff, review and guide philanthropic strategies at the hospital, and serve as high-level representatives to complement the CEO's role.

Get to know your hospital's clinicians and what is most important to them. Build connections with the various chiefs of the service or department chairs to review and approve progress toward fundraising goals and objectives, update the status of high-level prospects, review the chief's assignments and assigned prospects, and determine next steps of your work together.

Trusting

Build alignment and trust. Trust is an essential part of any successful relationship and is critical for building successful, lasting relationships. Without trust, doubt, uncertainty, and reservations will ruin any potential for alignment. Alleviate anxiety about encroachment on the physician-patient relationship. Break down barriers to trust. Work to avoid miscommunication. Allow clinicians to share their expectations, experiences, and ideas to encourage a relationship built on trust and communication. Building positive relationships between clinicians and philanthropy team is critical. Conduct an assessment of the current relationship and identify strengths and weaknesses that need to be addressed.

Address challenges at the earliest possible stage. Monitor the relationship and look for opportunities to constantly improve it. Host informal social gatherings to promote relationship growth. Create opportunities where clinicians can see firsthand the impact of their joint initiatives. Build alliances between the hospital and clinicians and create opportunities for success for both. Recognize and reward your clinicians.

Invest in Your Volunteer Leaders

While leading the $1 billion Discover the Difference, the largest campaign in the history of University Hospitals in Cleveland, I had the pleasure of working with Sheldon "Shelly" Adelman. Shelly was the Principal of Adelman Capital and once served as Chief Executive Officer of Blue Coral, one of the country's largest manufacturers of car-wash chemicals and waxes. Shelly was also the force and energy behind many successful startup companies. But more importantly, Shelly was one of the formidable board leaders who helped set and achieve University Hospital's inspiring campaign vision. He also became a pacesetting, major philanthropic investor during the silent phase of the campaign.

To me, Shelly was a mentor, teacher, and guide and I learned a great deal from him. He firmly believed in and helped lead a plan to promote volunteerism and get top-tier community leaders engaged. He knew this needed to be one of the first priorities of effective fundraising. And he knew how important a strong volunteer team was to implementing a fundraising plan, to advocating for the cause to the public, and to assisting with soliciting top-level prospects. Years later, I remain grateful to Shelly for teaching me that the success of any fundraising effort is directly related to the commitment of volunteer leaders and their determination to implement an effective fundraising plan.

Volunteer leadership that provides governance and strategic guidance for hospital fundraising is one of many key factors that determine the effectiveness of a hospital fundraising office's work. So, invest the time and attention to build, develop, and retain a group of highly qualified volunteer leaders.

Start at the top and build the volunteer leadership group intentionally. Develop customized and tailored job descriptions for each volunteer leadership position. Always be scanning the community for great volunteers and keep a flowing pipeline full of good candidates. And be aware of your volunteer leader's other obligations before inviting them to serve. The time and attention of top volunteers are enormously valuable, so be intentional about meeting and calling. Don't stalk them. Volunteer leaders appreciate you being genuine and up front with your intentions.

Before they join your volunteer program, let your volunteers know that you expect them to fundraise. And once you have your volunteers, reaffirm expectations. Know if you don't create a clear expectation of a culture of fundraising, you can't expect your volunteer leaders to become fundraising champions. And if possible, realize and discuss the alternatives to fundraising if your volunteer leader is unwilling to fundraise.

Volunteers want to be guided on what to do and how to do it. Convey to volunteers that they are representatives of the hospital fundraising office and that all of their actions, external and internal, help drive philanthropic investment. Provide an overview of the hospital fundraising and review policies and procedures, with an emphasis on those most likely to affect the work the volunteers are doing. Introduce hospital fundraising office staff in leadership positions and let each explain their role and relationship to volunteers. Host a strategic volunteer leader retreat to create a volunteer leader effectiveness improvement plan. Give opportunities for training and learning, and then allow people to decide which part of fundraising is a good fit for them.

Invest in Your Philanthropy Brand

In competitive markets, if companies do not show up, they remain unknown, unremarkable, and uncompetitive. Current and prospective philanthropic investors want information about what your hospital does and how successful you've been. They are also looking for information and evidence about what their investment did or will do and who or what they will affect. They want to confirm your impact and your value.

Make your presence known and build your hospital's philanthropy brand image. Highlight the achievements of your hospital, your clinicians, and your grateful patients. Show the breadth and depth of your philanthropic investors and everyone involved in achieving your hospital's mission. Generate interest and capture your philanthropic investor's attention by telling your hospital's story. Share what makes your hospital different from the rest. And keep your mission at the heart of the story.

And be sure you are "showing" and not merely "telling." Connect philanthropic investors to the actual people who are impacted by your mission: your hospital's grateful patients. Remember, content is king, and building personal connections helps to provide opportunities to prove value and relevance. Putting a face with the impact helps philanthropic investors become more inspired to help, and also allows them to share something personal. Empathy and personal connection are top reasons why people invest, fundraise, join an organization, or volunteer. Through stories and content, your fundraising office is able to communicate your hospital's achievements, connect with current and future philanthropic investors, and really share the impact you're making. Make your hospital relevant through storytelling. Help audiences understand what is important and why.

While what you show and tell your philanthropic investors is key, where you tell them is critical as well. You have to deliver content to philanthropic investors in the ways they are already consuming information. So create a beautiful, clean, engaging mobile-friendly website filled with stories, as well as concise and useful information that conveys how users can contribute. And because you know regular and frequent communication with your philanthropic investors is essential, make use of social media. Know that the more platforms your hospital uses, the more exposure it gains. Keep the demographics of your users in mind when deciding which social media platforms are right for your hospital. Keep your pages visual and dynamic and your audience engaged and involved. Remember that if your hospital does not have the resources to manage multiple social media channels, it's better just to pick one or two and manage them well.

Invest in Your Stewardship

Keeping your philanthropic investors happy is one of the key elements of a successful hospital fundraising office. Top hospital fundraising offices have an intense focus on working with philanthropic investors after they make large philanthropic investments. This is commonly the area where many hospital fundraising offices drop the ball, perhaps due to staff shortages or a one-dimensional focus on securing larger investments. But to achieve the highest levels of performance, make stewardship a leading priority.

If your philanthropic investors are not happy, they will not come back to you for repeat investments and, more importantly, they will also tell others about their negative experience with your fundraising office. Philanthropic investors having a poor experience can come down to many factors, such as a long wait for a thank you or acknowledgment, or overall poor communication. That's why best-practice hospital fundraising offices invest heavily in stewardship experience. They would go out of their way to ensure that their philanthropic investors receive the best stewardship possible.

In developing a philanthropy stewardship program, focus on recognizing, rewarding, communicating, and showing impact to ensure your philanthropic investors feel happy, valued, and motivated to invest again.

Recognize

Recognize the value of your philanthropic investors beyond simply their finances. Mail memorable thank-you letters. Remember a thank you is not merely a tax receipt. It should look like a personal letter from one friend to another, highlight the causes they care about, and celebrate their generosity. Your aspiration is to make your philanthropic investors feel like stars and heroes, because they are. And remember that amazing recognition is not just for large investments, but for investors at all levels.

Reward

Get to know your philanthropic investors more intimately and acknowledge the relationships and expertise they bring to the table by giving them a voice at your hospital.

Know that first impressions count and begin with a welcome packet to new philanthropic investors. Thank them early, frequently, and in a variety of ways. They are indispensable members of your hospital's team, so treat them extremely well. Pay attention and check-in with them from time to time. Take a sincere interest in what is happening in their life. Address their wants and needs. Spend time with them thinking and imagining what their philanthropy can accomplish and then illustrate for them how your hospital fundraising office can help them accomplish their goals, ambitions, wishes, and dreams.

Communicate

Philanthropic investors aren't just investing in your ideas, they're investing in your hospital, your vision, your impact, your value to the community. And while most philanthropic investors don't want to be involved in your hospital's day-to-day business operations, they appreciate updates on progress and take pride in your hospital's success. They'll be thrilled to hear about new clinician hires, partnerships, exciting patient stories, or noteworthy news. Provide both good and bad information promptly so your philanthropic investors feel like insiders in the know.

It's so important that your philanthropic investors don't view you as a "fund it and forget it" shop. Know that philanthropic investors will grow wary when there's too much silence. In the world of philanthropic investor stewardship, absence does not make the heart grow fonder. If you set the tone and establish the expectation for regular and valuable communication, your philanthropic investors will feel confident and be more willing to invest more in your hospital in the future.

Remember that communication is a two-way street. Listen to your philanthropic investors. Hear their underlying concerns. They want your hospital programs to succeed just as much as you do. So encourage open, clear dialogue so you can learn more about the philanthropic investments they are willing to make, the ones they will balk at, and the reasoning behind these decisions. Be amazed and surprised how much you can learn about your philanthropic investors by listening. Let your philanthropic investors tell you how they want to be further engaged with your hospital. Survey your philanthropic investors. Allow them to have a voice in how philanthropy works at your hospital.

And, as with all fundraising communications, produce quality over quantity.

Your philanthropic investors are almost certainly inundated with communications from the various nonprofits they support, so make your hospital stand out. Employ a well-thought-out, philanthropy-centric communications schedule. Nurture and cherish your relationship with your philanthropic investors by caring for them—send a highly personalized thank-you note as well as a formal, written thank-you note, midyear update, and an individualized, specific ask the following year. Send comprehensive reports, narratives, and articles to philanthropic investors on a recurring basis updating them about what has been done with their investment. Make certain your communications with philanthropic investors are varied, so they are getting a diversity of material about your hospital.

Show Impact

It's not about the money, it's about the positive impact created. Make certain your philanthropic investors appreciate where their investment is making an impact, where it is being spent, and the difference being made, because of them, at to your hospital and in the community. Underscore what your hospital can undertake and accomplish with and because of philanthropic investors, rather than giving them a litany of your hospital's achievements. Build a connection with them by being open, authentic, and honest about how your hospital is using philanthropic investment or where it is looking to improve and advance in the future.

\multicolumn{2}{c}{Five Components of Strategic Stewardship T.H.A.N.K. Your Philanthropic Investors!}	
T	Talk about Exceptionality
H	Handle Philanthropists Like Financial Investors
A	Apply Powerful Words of Praise
N	Note Often How They Are Changing the World
K	Keep Impact and Results Top of Mind

Five Components of Strategic Stewardship

We all have an idea of what strategic stewardship should look like. See the corresponding image. I suggest it is helpful to think about strategic stewardship in terms of five essential components:

Talk About Exceptionality

Don't be shy in telling your philanthropic investors what your hospital has accomplished. Differentiate your hospital. Communicate your hospital's strengths to stand out in a crowd. Be compelling. Make your message both personal and emotional. Get remembered. Illustrate your validity. Move your audience. Reward them for getting involved in big, excellent work, other than just writing a check. Demonstrate that you are using their investment wisely, for remarkable things. Move philanthropic investors to invest because they find your impact compelling and exceptional! Be creative. Make occasions, reports, and personal experiences affirming and inspiring.

Handle Philanthropists Like Financial Investors

Communicate the positive impact of their investment, the ROI. Show their investments are being used according to their intent. Appreciate generous financial investment. Say there are opportunities for their continued investment, resulting in greater returns! Talk investment, not donation. Demonstrating how you translate funds raised into change.

Apply Powerful Words of Praise

Don't just describe how you go about changing world, but why. Demonstrate how their philanthropic investments make a difference. Communicate from the end user's point of view. Don't lead with your hospital's needs. Fundraising often wrongly uses messaging of organizational need: "We need $50,000 to provide our patient services and programs." "We need $1 million to meet our endowment campaign goals." "We need to build a new hospital building." But that's not how to raise philanthropic investment effectively. To raise significant investments, nonprofits need to focus on how they translate money into social impact.

Note Often How They Are Changing World

Take end user's perspective. Talk about what the philanthropic investors will relate to. Show what has changed. Describe a moment of change in your philanthropy message. Philanthropic investors want to change the world! Celebrate success. Applaud accomplishment—not just yours, but theirs! Make it a celebration of the investor's philanthropic goals having been met. Impact drives income!

Keep Impact and Results Top of Mind

Philanthropic investors want to know that their money is being used effectively. So highlight the specific ways investments impact your hospital and community. Share what your organization is accomplishing. Share how your hospital is making progress and changing lives.

In conclusion, go beyond just recognizing individuals, engage them. Be creative about how to use resources to steward philanthropy. Integrate stewardship into your hospital fundraising office's culture. Strive to create and implement a best-in-class stewardship plan. Do the unexpected. Recognize that true gratitude will make all the difference.

Concentrate on appreciativeness and stewardship, not solicitation. Expend as much energy and effort into designing customized stewardship plans for philanthropic investors as you put into crafting moves management and solicitation plans. Your best future philanthropic investors are your current philanthropic investors, and if you overlook them or neglect to show how much you value and appreciate them, you run the risk of losing them.

Invest in Your Strategic Plan

Many healthcare philanthropy leaders walk around with a strategy locked in their heads. They know where their fundraising office needs to be and the key activities that will get it there. But oftentimes, the strategy is not written on paper, has not been communicated clearly or in detail, and few, if any, are acting on it. Without a clearly defined and articulated strategy, your hospital fundraising office may discover that import priority initiatives, the ones that drive the highest philanthropic return on investment, are receiving ancillary consideration or care.

But by developing your fundraising office's strategic plan, you can help provide your team and hospital leadership with a better idea of where your hospital fundraising office is running effectively and where it needs improvement. And when your hospital leaders, philanthropy staff, clinician partners, and even philanthropic investors know where you're going, you allow even greater opportunities for people to help you maximize your chances of getting there.

A strategic plan is extremely important for creating a strong, growing, and profitable hospital fundraising office. It's your road map for implementing and achieving your vision for the next three to five years. It clarifies your long-term goals and the steps necessary to attain them over the next two to five years. A solid hospital fundraising office strategic plan should

- use data to identify strategies for addressing issues that will arise over the next twelve months;
- establish priorities for your fundraising, making it easier to avoid distracting initiatives or projects;
- focus and align the energy, resources, and time of all involved with philanthropy;
- serves as a management tool that guides staff in prioritization and decision-making;
- define your understanding of success;
- act as a vehicle to communicate a common message; and
- measure activity and progress toward goals.

Strategic planning is not a set-it-and-forget-it exercise. Hospital fundraising offices need to revisit their strategy, monitor progress against milestones, and adjust to changing conditions. That means your strategic plan needs to be revised and adjusted regularly. So once you have a strategic plan in place, perform regular reviews, monitor progress against milestones, and adapt to changing conditions. These reviews of your strategic plan are an opportunity to take a step back, assess and evaluate the state of your fundraising and the industry, and realign your vision, goals, priorities, and action plan.

The nature and needs of your hospital will determine the timing and frequency of your fundraising office's strategic plan review process. For example, if your market changes rapidly, you might want to review your strategic plan more than once a year to keep pace. However, regardless of the interval you decide upon, you should be disciplined and ensure it happens regularly.

Finally, recognize that your fundraising office may have to persuade your hospital CEO or board chair to spend more on fundraising. Convince them with math. Use your strategic plan to show that if you do the math, it's clear that investing in fundraising operations will pay off for your hospital. The payoff can be startling.

To Recap

- Invest in the people most important to your success.
- Invest in your philanthropy brand.
- Invest in stewardship efforts.
- Invest in strategic planning for fundraising.

Chapter Five

Sustaining Value to Make a Profound Difference in the Health of Your Community

IN THIS CHAPTER

- Maintain a robust, future-focused vision
- Keep a continuous improvement and innovation mind-set
- Concentrate on remaining multidimensional
- Value people over money

When hospital fundraising leaders develop, invest in, and harness value within their hospital, positive results happen, and success becomes almost second nature. Regrettably, just because forward motion is happening, it is not guaranteed to continue. Therefore, not only must value be created, but a premium should be placed on sustaining it.

This chapter explains the fifth key driver to value-based healthcare philanthropy, sustaining value. To sustain value, you must seek to maximize the long-term success of your hospital and fundraising office by embracing continuing opportunities. It means discouraging short-term actions with negative long-term consequences. Having a "sustaining value" perspective requires a well-thought-out plan of action and discipline to stay focused on sustainable benefits and long-lasting contributions. It also means believing in investing in people and your hospital to enrich and make your community more healthy and vibrant.

Best-practice hospital fundraising offices resolve to make contemplative, long-term choices and connections to successfully sustain value. They make a profound difference in the health of their communities by maintaining a robust, future-focused, and well-documented vision. They keep alive a continuous improvement and innovation mind-set. They concentrate on remaining multidimensional. And they value people over money by cherishing diversity of thought, having high ethical standards, appreciating philanthropic investors, and treasuring people's relationships and networks.

Maintain a Robust, Future-Focused Vision

Perhaps the easiest thing to do to sustain value and momentum for your hospital and fundraising office is to keep raising the bar and keep momentum going by having a robust, future-focused vision. Creating a robust fundraising vision requires your hospital fundraising office to ask questions, make choices, and set priorities. It requires your operating leaders and your fundraising office to look at fundraising as an indistinguishable part of your hospital, not a separate function just generating money.

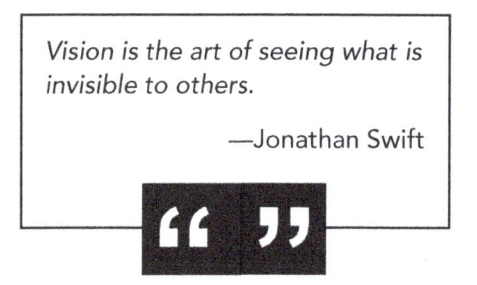

> *Vision is the art of seeing what is invisible to others.*
>
> —Jonathan Swift

Keep Setting out on a Great Challenge or Journey

Vision is your hospital's grounding force. It's the thing that unites everyone and ensures that all your efforts are moving the hospital in the same direction. The best fundraising vision really isn't even about money. It's about creating a program that maximizes the strengths of your hospital and seamlessly fits with what your hospital and your community want and need to accomplish. With this kind of vision, your hospital is seeking more than money; it is seeking investment and significant partners who want to change the world.

Ask Good Questions

A series of questions can help create a robust fundraising vision for your hospital. For describing need and purpose, ask the following:

- ◆ What are the pressing community health needs for your hospital to address?

- ◆ How is your hospital uniquely positioned to respond to these needs?

- What challenges will arise in your community over the next five years?

When describing your hospital's values, ask:

- What does your hospital care about?
- What are the most important services that your hospital should continue to provide, change, or begin to offer in the next five years?
- Should your hospital expand your services regarding the number of people served or should it deepen the level of service it currently gives to individuals and families?
- Will your hospital be serving the same people in five years as it is currently serving?
- What will be different? What will be the same?
- How will the world be improved if your hospital is successful in achieving its mission?
- What does your hospital want its philanthropic investors and community to do for it?
- Just invest money? Or is there some other way your hospital wants them involved in your mission?
- Can your hospital communicate with a great sense of opportunity and optimism and describe its plan for the future, its path for getting there, and the role of philanthropic investors in making the vision a reality?

Ask good questions.

Show the Way

Articulating your hospital's vision is vital to attracting philanthropic investment. So have a big dream or a great idea and be able to translate it to reality. Share your ideas and discover people who marvel in the opportunity and are willing to take the journey with you. They will make investments, provide support, and commit because they also want your vision to materialize, and they are glad someone is taking the lead. If your hospital's vision is clear and your community believes in it, your hospital and your fundraising will succeed.

Keep a Continuous Improvement and Innovation Mind-set

Several years ago, while I was working as a fundraiser at the Cleveland Clinic, I had the pleasure of working with Jack Kahl, a Cleveland area business leader and the visionary behind branding duct tape under the Duck® and Duck Tape® trademarks. Jack once handed me a plastic card the size of a credit card with his business logo on the front. On the back were fifteen points underlying his corporate culture. I remember reading through each one, and the card is still displayed in my office to this day. One of the fifteen points, in particular, has stuck with me and fits well here. It was, "Avoid a 'let's be average' mentality."

Being above average means doing what others won't or can't do. It means getting comfortable with what is uncomfortable, and it means above average hospital fundraising offices and the people that work in them love doing things they never thought they could even try. I truly believe being above average means you create your picture of success and make it a reality. It means being honest and specific as you consider where your hospital fundraising office is now and where you want it to be in the future, and determining what is needed to get from point A to point B. It means you maintain a mind-set of continuous improvement, improving process, and performance over time. It means you focus on activities that add value. It means eliminating energy drains, the things that drag down your hospital fundraising office. (And when you're dragged down, you're probably not

> ### Bold but Simple!
>
> Paint a picture. Keep your hospital's vision message bold but simple and explain it in such a way that even a twelve-year-old can understand it. Don't overcomplicate the message by including unnecessary scientific, medical-speak, or financial details that can be better shared later. Keep the focus only on key, simple messaging that illuminates the future your hospital has in mind to create. I often say it is imperative to create a "just imagine moment" and describe the ideal, depicting what the future would look like if their investment was made and vision fulfilled and showing what their lives or their community would be like. Share specifics and show a realistic, convincing future using visuals, diagrams, and pictures that help people visualize. When everyone sees the same picture, there is little room for different interpretations.
>
> **❗ important**

putting too much effort into your high-value efforts.) Yes, a continuous improvement and innovation mind-set means you think of delivering value—quality over quantity.

It also means your hospital fundraising office allows experimentation, makes room for creative approaches and fosters a positive working environment. It means eliminating unnecessary hard work, using evidence-based innovation, and testing new ideas. By adopting this mind-set, weaknesses and setbacks are only occasions to improve. It acknowledges that everything and everyone can grow and improve. This mind-set leads to greater fundraising success by having you make your goals consistent and strengthening your core competencies by investing in development and spending more time and money on those areas that are most important to your long-term success and growth. Again, please, never settle for being average. Your hospital fundraising office is better than that.

Concentrate on Remaining Multidimensional

To sustain value, don't put all your eggs in one basket. It's an old adage, but it still rings true. Being multidimensional means adopting a combination of engagement and outreach approaches, methods, and channels.

As a consultant specializing in hospital philanthropy, I've encountered many fundraising offices whose only fundraising outreach is through one or two standard approaches. Perhaps it is annual fund mail and/or special events. Or, they have concentrated most of their corporate philanthropy efforts on sponsorships for special events, galas, and golf outings. Maybe a 5K, a walk, or bike race is the focus. The crux this strategy is a failure to diversify. Seeking out multiple fundraising engagement and outreach approaches, methods, and channels to reach your potential philanthropic investors is critical to expanding the reach of philanthropy at your hospital.

A multidimensional fundraising plan is a necessity. This plan should include multiple engagement and outreach approaches, methods, and channels, such as

- capital campaigns;
- corporate sponsorships;
- cause marketing;
- digital online fundraising (website, mobile, email, social media, online crowds);

- direct mail fundraising;
- grants;
- grateful patients and families;
- major gift solicitation;
- recognition-driven membership campaigns;
- phonathons and telemarketing;
- planned philanthropy;
- principal philanthropy; and
- special events.

Your hospital fundraising office should not simply add approaches, methods, or channels just for the sake of having them. You should also strive to eliminate non-value-added channels and events. Do not host events for events' sake. Adopt a model of productivity, not activity. Work hard to determine what approaches, methods, and channels are unnecessary and eliminate or consolidate to add value.

A multidimensional strategy boils down to having a comprehensive approach for multiple, relevant audiences through a variety of engagement and outreach modes, platforms, and channels. Make sure all the parts, big or small, of your hospital fundraising office's strategy fit together. The key is to include all potential philanthropic investor audiences and to ensure compelling, targeted conversations, personal connections, or content reaches them in a wide variety of ways.

Value People over Money

George Wasmer is a successful Ohio business man and former president of a leading manufacturing supply company that I had the pleasure of working with on a fundraising campaign early in my career. George and his family are very well known for their philanthropy in their community. He is a compelling leader, and he was an early career mentor and advisor to me.

I remember watching George chair many meetings and making teams of volunteers and staff work well together toward fundraising goals. And, I remember him teaching me that to be a good professional fundraising leader you need to understand people, listen well, and in his words, "value people over money." Some of the most important things I learned in my career as a fundraising profession, I learned from people with experience, like George. And as a mentor and early guide, George helped me learn this important principle.

Human beings are social creatures by nature. Humans choose to live in communities, work in groups, develop families, and even form additional communities through churches, clubs, or support groups. Thus, to be effective at sustaining value, your hospital fundraising office must celebrate, include, and welcome all philanthropists, commit always to high ethical standards, make stewardship a perpetual top priority, network effectively, and value people over money.

Cherish Diversity

We all have differences, and recognizing, respecting, and cherishing those differences is a strategy to sustain value. Best-practice hospital fundraising offices welcome all philanthropists and value diversity. Conventionally, inclusion and diversity referred to people of different racial and ethnic backgrounds. Gender has also generally been included in the diversity classification. But now, inclusion and diversity encompass a much larger spectrum including life experiences, lifestyle choices, socioeconomic standing, and even sexual orientation. Therefore, a true commitment to inclusion and diversity is a multipronged approach that focuses on how to connect with multiple groups in a meaningful way.

Hospital philanthropy must be diverse to ensure that we are addressing the most important health and social problems in effective and culturally relevant ways. We appreciate today that top philanthropic investors in the United States are predominantly in the same demographic (white, age sixty plus, and male). Be cognizant that a homogenous group of philanthropic investors, composed of individuals with the same backgrounds and experiences, may produce a limited range of perspectives from which to draw inspiration. As we have said earlier, building value and sustaining it requires new ideas and approaches. Your ability to sustain value will be severely hindered if everyone thinks and acts alike.

So you must lead a diverse set of philanthropists to the table, fostering a culture of diverse philanthropy at your hospital that ensures that the funders of tomorrow are included, not just the funders of today. Create authentic access points and options that make getting involved less daunting. This means having candid, transparent conversations on how best to approach issues of inclusion and cultural diversity, gender diversity, and age diversity.

Advance Cultural Diversity

By embracing cultural diversity in healthcare, our hospital fundraising offices improve our overall value. Cultural diversity, also sometimes called multiculturalism, is the acceptance of the various cultural, racial, and ethnic groups. Best-practice hospital fundraising offices make it a practice to seek individuals from diverse backgrounds to be active participants in their hospital fundraising office's planning, design, implementation, and evaluation of philanthropy.

Promote Gender Diversity

Gender diversity is equitable or fair representation between genders. Best-practice hospital fundraising offices promote philanthropy and volunteer leadership opportunities equally with women and men. They applaud and celebrate the accomplishments of successful women in the same way that men's achievements usually are. They support and encourage women's philanthropy groups. They realize that vacant board seats or fundraising volunteer advisory committee roles are opportunities to address gender imbalance. They appreciate that a more gender diverse group makes their hospital fundraising office stronger and that getting more women interested in philanthropy programs at their hospital will have great benefits, both financially and otherwise. They take a proactive role in encouraging women to participate.

Encourage Age Diversity

Age diversity is the practice of including a full range of age groups. It addresses the generational differences of philanthropic investors. There are distinguishing characteristics sometimes described as the G.I. Generation, the baby boomers, Generation X, Generation Y, and millennials. Clearly, managing the likes and dislikes of philanthropic investors that span multiple generations represents tremendous challenges to hospital fundraising offices that want to be in tune with social trends, healthcare needs, and opinions on philanthropy, all of which are dynamics filtered through philanthropic investors' generational perceptions. Best-practice hospital fundraising offices understand that the key is recognizing that each generation brings to the table a variety of views and opinions on philanthropy and volunteerism.

They foster a sense of balance between fundraising approaches, making sure that their strategy is broad enough to reach all of the generations. For example, younger people want opportunities to make philanthropic investments online, and to get out into the field and roll up their sleeves. They appreciate that the younger generations of people are the ones who will build our future, so it is critical to start including them now.

Best-practice hospital fundraising offices continuously pull from a wide range of ages, experiences, and opinions. They also know the senior generations can offer a wealth of talent and time and have saved financial resources to make transformational impact.

> **Diversity of Thought**
>
> Thought diversity is appreciating and understanding that your philanthropic investors have different perspectives and a variety of ideas. One philanthropic investor's method for investing in your hospital or hospital program, for instance, might not be what you specifically envisioned or asked for—but it might be even better.
>
> **observation**

Be Strategic in Your Approach to Diversity

Consider using market research and measure who is making philanthropic investments and who is participating. Reflect and evaluate participation. Be open to the conversation and use your research to better understand the needs of your diverse community. Create a plan for how to recruit more diverse candidates. Track progress on diversity over time.

Ultimately, although individuals naturally form affinities with those who are like them, it's important to find a way to bring everyone to the same table so that the solutions for the community take into account all voices, needs, and abilities. Shape a collective vision and mutual participation. Truly embracing diversity means bringing about long-lasting change, rooted in authenticity to be successful. Find a way to celebrate our differences and similarities as a community.

Keeping High Ethical Standards

Valuing people over money is also about keeping high ethical standards. In order to be successful, your hospital fundraising office must achieve and maintain a high level of public trust and respect. To do this, your fundraising office must pattern the highest standard of ethical behavior and ensure that its actions reflect a commitment to ethical practices. At a minimum, this means providing a simple and risk-free method to report anonymously actions that may be fraudulent, dishonest, or illegal.

Best-practice hospital fundraising offices use the Donor Bill of Rights developed by industry experts at the Association of Fundraising Professionals (AFP), Association for Healthcare Philanthropy (AHP), Council for Advancement and Support of Education (CASE), and The Giving Institute. The bill aims to ensure that philanthropy merits the respect and trust of the public. It also gives current and future philanthropic investors confidence in your hospital fundraising office.

The Donor Bill of Rights states that all quality nonprofits should provide their philanthropic investors the following rights:

1. To be informed of the organization's mission
2. To be informed of those serving on the governing board
3. To have access to the organization's most recent financial statement
4. To be assured their gifts will be used for the purposes for which they were intended
5. To receive appropriate acknowledgment and recognition
6. To be assured that information about their donations is handled with respect and confidentiality
7. To expect professional relationships with individuals representing organizations
8. To be informed whether those seeking donations are volunteers, employees, or hired solicitors
9. To have the opportunity for their names to be deleted from mailing lists that an organization may intend to share
10. To feel free to ask questions when making a donation

Never Treat People as Numbers

Never lose touch with the human side of hospital fundraising, especially as we move into a world of increased technological connectivity. It is people who work for our hospital fundraising offices, so invest in your hospital's people and programs. Never treat people as numbers, metrics, and the bottom line. When a hospital fundraising office starts regarding people simply as totals on a spreadsheet, or numbers on an annual fund mailing list, it becomes disconnected from those people. Nothing makes a philanthropic investor feel less appreciated than making them feel like just a number.

Each philanthropic investor is exceptional and unique. They, or a loved one, have most likely had a medical experience at your hospital. They have had positive days. They have had difficult days. They have felt helpless and vulnerable. The have been adamant, unmovable, and strong. They have had highs and lows. They have had times where they want to shout with delight and days where they cry with sorrow. Never forget that they are real, thinking, and feeling human beings.

Make People Feel Happy to Join Your Hospital's Cause

Exude charisma and radiate magnetism that inspires confidence. Be positive, engage people, and make them want to be around your hospital. Speak with confidence and conviction. Love what you do. Look people in the eye when you're talking to them. Don't glance around the room, check your phone or your watch, or look everywhere but at them. Engage them with your eyes, not just your voice. Make people feel special.

Be Prompt and Professionally Savvy

Be prompt and professionally savvy, especially with thank-you letters and receipts. If you thank people late, produce a vague or impersonal report, or overpromise and underdeliver, your philanthropic investors will talk negatively about you in the community, give you lousy feedback, and will think twice before investing in you again.

Pay Attention to Detail

Even something as minor as an incorrect salutation or misspelled name on an invitation or thank-you note or pledge reminder will give the impression that you don't respect or value the investor or their investment enough to get that right. Paying attention to detail, even when details may seem mundane to you, can mean the difference between having a loyal philanthropic investor who tells ten people how wonderful you are, or having a previous philanthropic investor who tells one hundred people how awful your hospital fundraising office's stewardship is. To sustain value, pay attention to details. It is the details that matter when aiming to provide a stellar philanthropic investor experience. Stand apart by greeting philanthropic investors by their name, always; following up when promised; reaching out when a significant event happens; and spell-check all correspondence before being distributed.

Be Quick to Respond

Answer questions and inquiries from philanthropic investors as soon as possible. Create protocols that encourage responsiveness. Allocate sufficient resources to make this a priority. Know that if your hospital philanthropy office isn't responsive, your philanthropic investors will find an office that is.

Treat Unsatisfied Philanthropic Investors with Careful Attention

Know your hospital fundraising office will come across dissatisfied philanthropic investors. Restore confidence, solve problems, always keep the right attitude—a combination of caring, empathy, and urgency. Apologize and find a compromise if a philanthropic investor is unsatisfied. It's much easier than fighting with them over what they thought you didn't do or deliver.

You will find that there are some people you just can't please no matter how hard you try or what you do, so move those types of philanthropic investors as fast as you can and get on with your fundraising rather than let them stew and argue. Don't let a few dollars ruin your fundraising; just chalk it up and move on. And always remember, your hospital fundraising office is a brand ambassador for the hospital you work for.

Simple touches really have a big impact. Always focus on the people behind the numbers to sustain value. Show people that your hospital fundraising office is always listening to them—going above and beyond to provide them with stellar experiences—and cares about them as individuals more than money.

Treasure People's Relationships and Networks

In 2006, when working with University Hospitals in Cleveland, Ohio, I was given a copy of Keith Ferrazzi's book, *Never Eat Alone,* by a philanthropic investor and leading member of the health system's board. The board member told me how his and his sales team's success as connectors and networkers helped create a successful business. He said he thought the key to successful fundraising was also effective networking—developing genuine connections versus meeting a fundraising goal. He thought sharing the book with me would be helpful. It was, very. Ferrazzi is an author, business leader, and networking expert, and the book was based on his personal networking experiences. Ferrazzi understood real networking was about finding ways to make other people more successful. I interpreted his lesson as focusing first upon how I could benefit others, rather on than how others could benefit me. And I have applied this often in my daily professional life.

Networking is the simple concept of developing and maintaining meaningful relationships with those who have similar interests. It is valuing people and relationships over money. And it is about building relationships with trust and value. The real lesson here is that to sustain value in value-based philanthropy, your hospital fundraising team needs to form relationships that mean something and that focus on how it can help others, not on how people can help your hospital and its fundraising. Position your fundraising office as a place that can solve problems, open doors, and that does not expect anything in return. Fundamentally, it's about people and relationships, so your hospital fundraising office should strive to be a valuable hub in the middle of your community.

Be Committed

As a final point, I recommend you be very committed and intentional. No matter what your hospital fundraising office's goals are, or how difficult they'll be to achieve, sustaining value starts with commitment. Commit to at least one of the ideas above and you will begin to maximize long-term success. Then take on the next idea, and then another one. Commitment is what has shaped some of the most successful hospitals and health systems. Commitment is what turns an average performer into an extraordinary one. Commitment to sustaining is what spurs an ordinary hospital fundraising office to achieve extraordinary success and make a profound difference in the health of their community.

To Recap

- Maintain a robust, future-focused vision.
- Keep a continuous improvement and innovation mind-set.
- Concentrate on remaining multidimensional.
- Value people over money.
- Be committed.

Chapter Six

Concluding Thoughts

IN THIS CHAPTER

- ⇢ Do better, not just more
- ⇢ Be transparent
- ⇢ Embrace change
- ⇢ Do good and have fun

The reasoning behind value-based healthcare is about focusing on the continuum of care for patients rather than episodes of care. It focuses on being proactive, up front, and honest with information so patients can make informed decisions. It rewards clinicians for the value of the care, not the number of services they provide, and it focuses on people, not money.

Similarly, my philosophy of value-based philanthropy also focuses on a continuum, one of association—a consistent relationship, rather than episodic meetings, irregular fundraising appeals, or occasional correspondences or contacts with potential or current philanthropic investors. It also focuses on connection, value, and people, not money.

Throughout this book, I have offered my recommendations for demonstrating your hospital's value to clearly show impact, maximizing the value of core programs, measuring value to ensure high performance, investing in value to build an amazing hospital fundraising office, and sustaining value to make a profound difference. These five key drivers of value-based philanthropy are key to building an effective organization.

And as a final recommendation, I suggest you continuously seek opportunities for four additional and valuable pursuits:

- ◆ Be productive, not just active
- ◆ Be transparent
- ◆ Embrace change
- ◆ Do good while having fun

Be Productive, Not Just Active

Contrary to Nike's "Just do it" slogan, I recommend you don't just do it, but rather do what needs to be done. To be value based, it's critical to know where to focus your attention and efforts. The question is: What is the best use of your time, and are you being productive or merely active? Being active is getting things done; being productive is getting the right things done using evidence-based methods to achieve better outcomes. Focus on quality rather than quantity and always focus on value. Advance value and you will advance philanthropic investments.

Be Transparent

Transparency is perhaps one of the most important aspects of hospital fundraising. It raises philanthropic investors' confidence and builds trust, and confidence and trust are the basis of all important relationships. Your philanthropic investors must trust you. Recognize that if your hospital fundraising office isn't open, honest, and transparent, it cannot build confidence and trust. Be open and honest with philanthropic investors if you want them to invest their hard-earned money into your hospital.

Publish your results and accounts in an accessible and straightforward way to demonstrate your transparency. Provide transparency on salaries and expenses, and provide a timely and comprehensive response to any salary or spending inquiry. Focus on the activities that matter to the public, the ones that directly relate to your philanthropic investors' interest in your hospital's mission. Spend time giving details and validating that what you are doing is in your hospital's mission's best interest. Let philanthropic investors know what their investment will be used for, why it will help your hospital's mission, and how it improved society or someone's life.

All things considered, know that the more transparent you are, the more criticism you will attract. Don't be afraid of evaluation, questioning, or the probing that may happen. Welcome critical review.

Embrace Change

In healthcare, external market factors impact the pace of change. The big change factors are the speed at which the healthcare market is changing, the growth changes in populations, the advances in technology, the shifts in demographics, including age, gender, and socioeconomic status, the health coverage shifts, both the private and public markets, and lastly, politics!

The word *Kaizen* is the Japanese word for a "good change" (Kai = change, Zen = good). It is a recognized business philosophy that concentrates on promoting continual improvement and embracing positive change. So practice kaizen—replace conventional fixed ideas with fresh ones, question current practices and standards, think of how to overcome barriers, not why something cannot be done, advance implementation not perfection, and correct something right away if a mistake is made. This is what it means to embrace change.

Embracing change means continuously striving to develop and understand your hospital fundraising office's own unique performance culture. It means bringing in people, ideas, and resources that either sustain your performance culture or add value to it. Be a strategic thinker, be very supportive of others, and be creative.

And Finally, Do Good While Having Fun

My father, William Herbert Mountcastle, spent thirty years with the Glidden Paint Company as a regional sales manager responsible for overseeing sales and sales strategy within an assigned market of Ohio and some parts of Michigan. He was a fantastic dad and a hardworking professional. He passed away Memorial Day weekend in 2013, three months after I started my consulting business. I had the pleasure while growing up of watching him lead, direct, and generate new business and maintain existing accounts for the paint company. He worked hard to build and keep great relationships with individuals and their family-owned, traditional hardware stores and then individual buyers at mass merchandisers as the profitable do-it-yourself trend moved through the retail industry. He put people first and took a value-based approach to his work.

When he retired from Glidden in 1998, he took leadership, as a volunteer executive director, of a local church hunger center. He went from selling paint to helping a group of dedicated church volunteers achieve a mission of feeding hungry people and working to solve hunger issues in my west-side Cleveland, Ohio neighborhood. As director, he provided administrative leadership and support. He championed fundraising and philanthropy and invited local business leaders and politicians to become partners in the fight against hunger in our community. He led volunteers to help sort and pack food donations. He coordinated home and community center deliveries. He planned food collection events during Thanksgiving and Christmas holidays. And he enjoyed it. He was doing good and having fun. Not surprising, because this was one of the many important life lessons he taught me, and my two sisters, over the years.

My dad had many colorful sayings like, "Don't burn your bridges," "Are you investing?" "What does your point have to do with the price of eggs in China?" "If your friend jumped off a bridge, would you?" and many more. But one saying really stuck, probably because he said it so often: "Do good and have fun." When I would leave the house as a teenager, step onto a sports field to compete, head off to college for the first time, drive to the church to be married, take one of my two newborn daughters home from the hospital, or take on a new job as a healthcare fundraising consultant, he would say it. He seemed to know this simple message could apply to so many situations, so he said it often to me.

To Recap

And so I conclude this book on hospital fundraising with my dad's simple words of advice, my interpretations of what it means today, and how it applies to you, an advocate and promoter of value-based healthcare philanthropy. And my interpretation of how my dad's advice applies to healthcare philanthropy is that all of us must

- ◆ become champions for those things that make our world a better, healthier place;
- ◆ take action to make sure that help is available to those who need it;
- ◆ volunteer time and talents to a worthy cause;
- ◆ work harder, more consistently, and smarter than anyone else;
- ◆ seek new and better ways to do what you do;
- ◆ speak up in support of things that make your community better;
- ◆ make philanthropic investments if you can;

- celebrate the magnificence of philanthropy and volunteers, no matter the type or size of investment or amount of time volunteered; and, most importantly

- do good and have fun.

Index

A

accountants, 29–30
acquisition mailings, 45
Adelman, Sheldon "Shelly", 62
Affordable Care Act (ACA), 14, 57
allied professionals, 29–30
annual fund, 44
annual fund mail, 75
annual fund mailing list, 80
annual goals, 29
annual philanthropy, 50
annual philanthropy report, 23–24
annual self-assessments, 36
asking, 22, 25–26, 31, 48
Association for Healthcare Philanthropy (AHP), 34, 54–55, 80
  research, 54
Association of Fundraising Professionals (AFP), 55, 80
attorneys, 29–30

B

baby boomers, 28, 78
bequests, 29, 54
best-practice approaches, 9
best-practice hospital fundraising offices, 25, 27, 30, 42, 44, 48, 54, 65, 71, 78–80

board, 36, 80
  high-performance, 36
board chair, 70
board member, 82
board nominations, 8
budgets, fundraising communication's, 45
building relationships, 2, 27, 58, 83

C

Campbell, Julia, 13
Canfield, Jack, 26
capital campaigns, 75
case, 12, 15
case statement, 15–16
CEO, 36, 58–59
CharityChannel's Quick Guide to Developing Your Case for Support, 16
clinicians, 4, 13, 35–39, 48, 54, 59–62, 64
communications, 8, 23–24, 32, 45, 58, 61–62, 66
  planned, 23
community health, 3, 14–15, 19, 41, 72
community health needs assessment (CHNA), 14–15
community leaders, 12, 17

community partnerships, 21–22, 35, 39
confidentiality, 34, 80
continuous improvement, 71–72, 74–75, 83
conversion rate, 47, 49
corporate charitable giving, 39
corporations, 31, 35, 38–39
Cost per dollar raised (CPDR), 44
costs, 7, 23, 25–26, 44
cross-departmental support, 8
cultivation, 27–28, 46–47
culture, 34, 36, 45, 54–55, 63, 77
   hospital fundraising office's, 68
   philanthropy-focused fundraising, 55

D

demonstrating value, 3–4, 6, 11, 16, 18
differentiators, 6–7
   hospital's, 3–4, 6, 20
discrimination, 34
diversity, 67, 72, 77–79, 87
   cultural, 77–78
Donor Bill of Rights, 80
Drucker, Peter, 41
Dunlop, David, 46

E

ethical behavior, 79
event philanthropic investments, 49
events, 9, 11, 31, 39, 49, 76
   special, 75–76
expenses, total fundraising, 44

F

Fazio, Victor, 59
federally qualified health centers (FQHCs), 18
feedback, 17–18, 57
financial planners, 29–30
Ford, Henry, 26
fundraisers, 28, 37, 42, 44, 47–49, 55–57, 74
   hospital's, 4
   hospital's top, 59
fundraising, peer-to-peer, 49
fundraising communications, 24, 35, 66
   hospital's, 35
fundraising net, total, 44
fundraising office, 13, 25, 32, 37–38, 42–47, 50–51, 53–54, 57, 60–61, 64–65, 69–72, 75, 79, 83
fundraising operations, 25–26, 42, 70
fundraising silos, 8
fundraising staff, 44, 54–55

G

Getting Started in Charitable Gift Planning: Your Guide to Planned Giving, 29
Getting Started in Prospect Research: What You Need to Know to Find Who You Need to Find, 33
grateful patient philanthropic investments, 33, 49
grateful patient program, 36–37, 45, 61
grateful patient referrals, 48–49
grateful patients, 9, 12–13, 31, 33, 36, 38, 60, 64, 76
   engaging, 36
grateful patients as storytellers, 13
grateful patient stories, 12
groups, women's philanthropy, 78

H

Hancks, Meredith, 33
healthcare philanthropy, 26, 55, 88
　value-based, 2, 71, 88
healthcare philanthropy consultant, 11
healthcare philanthropy leaders, 69
Health Insurance Portability and Accountability Act (HIPAA), 34–35, 50, 61
high-capacity philanthropic investors, 32–33
hospital CEO, 57, 70
hospital employee philanthropic investment, 31
hospital employees, 10, 27, 29–31
hospital fundraising, 5, 8, 28, 34, 43, 63, 80, 86, 88
hospital fundraising fundamentals, 22
hospital fundraising industry, 48
hospital fundraising leaders, 22, 57, 71
hospital fundraising office, 21–25, 27, 30, 34, 37–38, 41, 44–51, 53–55, 57–59, 61, 63, 65, 69–70, 72, 74–80, 82–83, 85–87
hospital fundraising office employee handbook, 35
hospital fundraising offices, highest-performing, 54
hospital fundraising office's goals, 83
hospital fundraising office's planning, 78
hospital fundraising office's strategy, 76
hospital fundraising office staff, 63
hospital fundraising process, 5
hospital fundraising teams, 2, 42, 46, 83
hospital leaders, 10–11, 15, 18, 36, 42, 57, 69
hospital leadership, 10, 24, 39, 69
hospital philanthropy, 75, 77
hospitals, best-practice, 8–9, 11–12, 17–19, 22, 24, 27, 43
hospital's brand, 6, 8
hospital's fundraising, 22, 39
hospital's fundraising office, 21, 25, 35, 59
hospital's mission, 5, 7, 15–16, 27, 29, 32, 35, 44, 64, 86
hospital's online philanthropy page, 50
hospital's value, 3–7, 9, 11, 13–15, 17, 19, 42, 73, 85

I

insurance consultants, 29–30
investors, 5, 24, 27, 29, 45, 65, 81
　approach philanthropic, 19
　asking philanthropic, 22
　connect philanthropic, 64
　dissatisfied philanthropic, 82
　employee philanthropic, 31
　external philanthropic, 30
　greeting philanthropic, 81
　guide philanthropic, 50
　hospital's philanthropic, 5, 28
　loyal philanthropic, 81
　moving, 47, 67
　new, 25
　prospecting philanthropic, 32
　successful philanthropic, 5
　top philanthropic, 13, 60, 77
　transition philanthropic, 50

J

journalists, 10

K

Kahl, Jack, 74
KPIs (key performance indicators), 42–44, 50

L

leaders
  compelling, 76
  corporate, 33
  formidable board, 62
  local business, 88
  nurse, 36
Legal Aid Society, 18
levels, hospital's philanthropy, 24

M

major gift officers, 50
marketing, 8, 12, 75
marketing communications, 7–8
Medicaid, 11
metrics, 41–43, 46–49, 80
  activity, 41, 43, 46, 51
  advanced, 50
  classic, 43
  monitoring philanthropic investment level, 41, 43, 48, 51
millennials, 78
Mountcastle, William Herbert, 87

N

new philanthropic investors, 11, 21–22, 33, 39, 45–46, 65

O

online philanthropy, 48–49

P

participation rates, peer-to-peer event fundraising, 48–49
patient philanthropy, 34
  grateful, 60
patients, 2, 4–7, 12–13, 15, 17, 19, 32–34, 37–38, 41, 49–50, 60–61, 85
  hospital's, 32–33
patient stories, grateful, 12–13, 16
perception of value, 3–4, 19–20
performance metrics
  classic fundraising, 41, 43, 51
  unique, 41, 43, 48, 51
personal connections, 57, 64, 76
PHI (protected health information), 34–35
philanthropic goals, 24, 28, 38
philanthropic investments, 3–4, 10, 12, 15–16, 22–33, 36–38, 43, 46–50, 54, 58, 60, 66–68, 73, 79, 86, 88
  average size, 47–48
  large, 65
  new, 31, 35
  repeated, 25
philanthropic investor numbers, 45
philanthropic investor pool, 45–46
philanthropic investors, 2–28, 30–34, 36, 38–39, 42, 44–48, 50, 53, 55, 59, 62, 64–69, 72–73, 77–82, 85–86
philanthropic investor transfers, 48, 50
philanthropic priorities, 13, 24, 26, 61
philanthropic results, hospital's, 53

philanthropic return, highest, 69
philanthropists, 67-68, 77
philanthropy, 23-24, 26-27, 29-31, 36-38, 43, 46, 49-50, 58-61, 65, 69, 75-76, 78, 88-89
philanthropy brand, 53, 63, 70
philanthropy-centric communications schedule, 66
philanthropy experience, 25-26
philanthropy programs, 61, 78
　employee, 31
　hospital employee, 30-31
　planned, 30
physicians, 7, 10, 15, 17, 25, 34, 36, 41, 60-61
planned giving, 29
planned philanthropic investments, 29-30
planned philanthropic investment vehicles, 29
planned philanthropy, 27-29, 54, 76
potential philanthropic investors, 20, 27, 30, 75
privacy, 34-36, 50
process, hospital fundraising office's onboarding, 34
professionals, allied, 29-30
profile, hospital's, 9-11
prospecting, 22, 32-33
protected health information (PHI), 34-35

R

raising philanthropic investment, 44, 60
recognition, 20, 23-24, 39, 65, 80
recognition societies, 23-24, 29

relationships, 9, 15, 24, 26, 28, 37, 39, 57, 60, 62-63, 65-66, 83, 86-87
　clinician-patient, 37
reputation, 6-7, 9, 15
retention, 25, 44-45
retention rate of philanthropic investors (RRPI), 25, 44-45

S

Sagrestano, Brian, 29
social media, 32, 64, 75
software, 45
　wealth screening, 33
solicitation, 22, 27-28, 46-47, 68
standards, high ethical, 72, 77, 79
stewardship, 26, 45, 47, 55, 64-65, 68, 77
　hospital fundraising office's, 81
　strategic, 67
stories
　compelling, 13
　inspiring, 13
　intimate, 19
　phony, 13
storytelling, 13, 64
Storytelling in the Digital Age: A Guide for Nonprofits, 13
strategic plan, 7-8, 25, 54, 69-70
strategies, digital engagement, 49
sustain value, 71-72, 75, 77, 81-83

T

technology, 6, 17, 32, 57-58, 87
top hospital fundraising offices, 60, 64
top hospital leadership, 54, 57
transparency, 86
trust officers, 29-30

U

university hospitals, 62, 82

V

value-based philanthropy, 2, 83, 85
vision, 15, 35, 66, 69-70, 72-74
  best fundraising, 72
  collective, 79
  common, 59
  future-focused, 71-72, 83
  hospital's, 73
  robust fundraising, 72
  well-documented, 72
volunteer committee, 30
volunteering, 10
volunteerism, 62, 78
volunteer leader retreat, strategic, 63
volunteer leaders, 42, 54, 62-63
  qualified, 63
  strong community, 35
volunteer leadership, 63
volunteer leadership opportunities, 78
volunteer leadership position, 63
volunteer program, 63
volunteers, 7, 30, 32, 35-36, 54, 63-64, 76, 80, 87-89
volunteer time, 88

W

Wahlers, Robert, 29
Wasmer, George, 76
wealth, intergenerational shifts, 28
Wooden, John, 21

Did you know that CharityChannel Press is the fastest growing publisher of books for busy nonprofit professionals? Here are some of our most popular titles.

CharityChannel.com/bookstore

CharityChannel PRESS

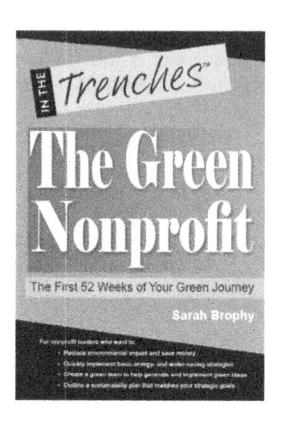

CharityChannel.com/bookstore

CharityChannel
PRESS

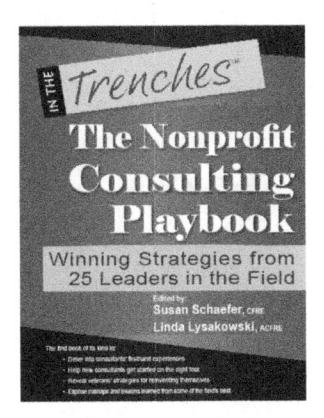

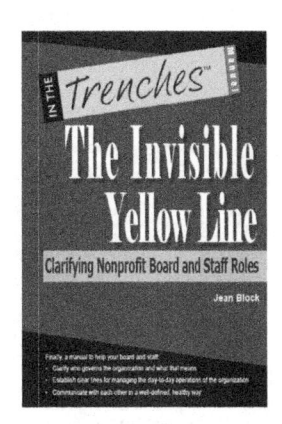

CharityChannel.com/bookstore

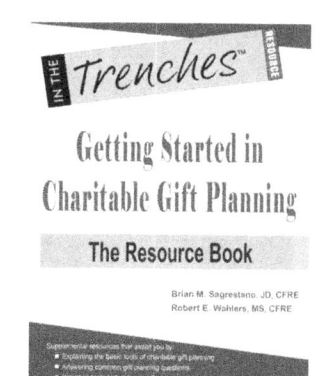

And more!

CharityChannel.com/bookstore

CharityChannel PRESS

Made in the USA
Las Vegas, NV
27 December 2023